William Sh

JA 2 5 16

THE
WINTER'S TALE

edited by Kenneth Branagh

822.33
R 3
SHA

BARRINGTON AREA LIBRARY
505 N. NORTHWEST HWY.
BARRINGTON, ILLINOIS 60010

NICK HERN BOOKS
www.nickhernbooks.co.uk

www.branaghtheatre.com

A Nick Hern Book

This edition of *The Winter's Tale* first published in Great Britain in 2015 as a paperback original by Nick Hern Books Limited, The Glasshouse, 49a Goldhawk Road, London W12 8QP, in association with the Kenneth Branagh Theatre Company

This edition of *The Winter's Tale* copyright © 2015 Kenneth Branagh
Introduction and Interviews copyright © 2015 Kenneth Branagh Theatre Company
Sheet Music copyright © 2015 Patrick Doyle

Cover image © Johan Persson and Shaun Webb Design

Designed and typeset by Nick Hern Books, London
Printed in the UK by CPI Group (UK) Ltd

A CIP catalogue record for this book is available from the British Library

ISBN 978 1 84842 540 8

MIX
Paper from responsible sources
FSC
www.fsc.org
FSC® C013604

Contents

'It is required you do awake your faith…':
Shakespeare's 'Old Tale'
Russell Jackson

The first recorded performance of *The Winter's Tale* was given by Shakespeare's company, the King's Men, at the Globe in 1611. It was seen by King James in the same year and was given seven times at Court between then and 1640. Shakespeare's source was the prose romance by Robert Greene, *Pandosto*, subtitled 'The Triumph of Time', first published in 1588. A king loses the ability to distinguish delusion from reality, veers into tyranny (the word is used more than once), and becomes the opposite of the ideal ruler James I aspired to be. Shakespeare's play uses important elements of Greene's romance, altering some aspects of the plot and adding three new characters: Antigonus, Paulina, and the trickster Autolycus, the 'snapper up of unconsidered trifles'. It mixes psychological trauma, cruelty and heartbreak with nostalgia and comedy. At once realistic and a fantasy, the play includes reminders that its events, considered with any degree of scepticism, would be 'hooted at' as 'an old tale' – that is, the kind of far-fetched story that might be told to children, with all the appropriate mixture of terrors and reassurance that we associate with fairy stories. At the same time, as in some popular fairy stories, it allows for the collateral damage that accompanies many happy endings.

The tale that might be told by a winter fireside – 'a sad tale's best for winter' – also encompasses ideas about nature and time (both capable of being either benevolent or destructive) that reach beyond the realm of simple explanation. In that respect it is a play of mystery, with characters expressing wonder from the very first scenes at events and behaviour that are either exceptionally promising or, as the play develops, extremely harmful. The ideal relationship of the Sicilian king Leontes and his queen Hermione, and between them and Polixenes, king of Bohemia – whom Leontes has not seen since childhood – is threatened by an inexplicable and apparently sudden mental aberration on Leontes' part. He accuses Hermione of adultery with Polixenes and imprisons her to await trial, despite the fact that she is pregnant. The loyal courtier Camillo, instructed to poison Polixenes, instead warns him of the danger to his life and joins him in fleeing to Bohemia. In prison, Hermione gives birth to a daughter – Perdita – and when the formidable lady Paulina brings the child to him, Leontes insists that it should be burnt to death. Nevertheless, he relents to the extent of instructing Antigonus to take the child to some desert place and abandon it.

As a concession, Leontes has determined that the Oracle of the god Apollo should be consulted. Its answer is brought at the beginning of the queen's trial: not only is Hermione vindicated against the accusation of adultery, but the paternity of the young prince Mamillius is confirmed and Leontes denounced as a 'jealous tyrant'. When he defiantly declares that 'there is no truth in the Oracle', news arrives almost immediately of the death of the young prince. Hermione collapses, and is carried offstage. She is presently reported to have died from the shock. Grief-stricken and penitent, Leontes resolves to mourn both wife and child.

Fulfilling his mission of relative mercy, Antigonus reaches the coast of Bohemia and leaves the child there, with information that will identify it, together with gold that may somehow ensure its prosperity should it survive. The dream that Antigonus describes before he places the infant and the bundle tenderly on the ground ('Blossom, speed the well') suggests to him that this is indeed the daughter of Polixenes, a misinterpretation that is of a piece with the play's emphasis on what should or should not be believed: 'Dreams are toys,' he reflects, 'Yet for this once, yea superstitiously, / I will be squared by this.' For all he knows Hermione has 'suffered death' (he was not present at the trial) and her appearance in the dream, as if she were a ghost, would seem to indicate this.

The prophecy that he will never see his wife Paulina again is fulfilled almost immediately: a storm comes on, and before he can make his escape, Antigonus is attacked and eaten by a bear.

This is the pivotal sequence of the play, which tilts into comedy with the arrival on stage of the old shepherd looking for his sheep. The shepherd immediately assumes that the abandoned baby is the result of an illicit love affair: 'They were warmer that got this than the poor thing is now.' When his son arrives, full of the excitement of seeing two astonishing events, a ship lost with all hands and an old gentleman being eaten by a bear, the old shepherd acknowledges that these are 'heavy matters' but points out 'Thou met'st with things dying, I with things new-born.' It is in the nature of stories like this for audiences to expect some kind of pleasing outcome to the Oracle's enigmatic statement that 'The king shall live without an heir if that which is lost be not found.' At least one part of that prophecy has been fulfilled. Quite how it will be completed is far from clear. It will be sixteen years before this resolution will be achieved, a 'wide gap' too long for most plays but achieved here with impressive effrontery by Shakespeare, with the help of Time – in person.

Time shares with both Nature and the playwright the power to 'please some' and 'try all', bringing 'both joy and terror'. Both Time and Shakespeare are able to 'o'erthrow Law, and in one self-born hour / To plant and o'erwhelm custom.' Like Shakespeare, Time calls for what Coleridge famously called a 'willing suspension of disbelief' – or rather, Time claims with good-humoured finality the ability to *impose* it, as part of the contract between the audience and the play. This, then, is 'an old tale', a reminder that wonders may never cease, in which characters within the play express their astonishment and incredulity on our behalf. For us, as for them, it is required that, for our pleasure's sake, we 'do awake our faith'.

Jealousy, Greene points out in *Pandosto*, is unique among the passions of the mind in placing the sufferer beyond the persuasion of friends or the effects of time: he is 'always frozen with fear and fired with suspicion' because 'that wherein consisteth all his joy' has become 'the breeder of his misery'.

In *The Winter's Tale*, as in the tragedy *Othello*, Shakespeare presents male sexual jealousy as destructive, taking the sufferer beyond reason and isolating him. In the psychological theories of the time it is a variety of 'melancholy'. Perception becomes distorted and delusions take over, as though in a dream or nightmare. Accused of adultery, Hermione tells Leontes, 'My life stands in the level of your dreams,' and his chilling, unanswerable reply is 'Your actions are my dreams.' But this irrational state, like other natural occurrences in the play, is also part of what Perdita describes as 'great creating Nature'. There is nothing surprising (or original) in the suggestion that Nature encompasses 'things dying' and 'things new-born': what is surprising is the way *The Winter's Tale* reminds us of this, notably in Perdita's comments on hybrid flowers in Act Four, but also implicitly in the fact that a storm and a wild carnivore are no less part of Nature than its more benign aspects. Shadowing these references in the play is Nature's relationship with Art, in a complex of ideas that finds its fullest expression later in *The Tempest* with the figure of Prospero, the magus, exiled duke and, in the last analysis, playwright and actor on both the stage and the play's fictional island.

The restorative effect of the pastoral world in Act Four, and the love of Polixenes' son Florizel for Perdita, 'now grown in grace / Equal with wondering', echo the childhood innocence of the two kings evoked by Polixenes in Act One: 'We were as twinned lambs that did frisk i' th' sun... What we changed was innocence for innocence.' Although the idyll is threatened by the Bohemian king's anger at his son's underhand wooing of a shepherd's daughter, in this case what was earlier called 'the doctrine of ill-doing' does not prevail. Rather, a solution is achieved through the revelation of Perdita's true identity and the reconciliation of Leontes and Polixenes. The astonishing revelation that Hermione did not die is accomplished not simply through report but also by the seeming magic of a statue that lives and breathes – and is indeed not a magical effect but the queen herself.

Is there any significance in the fact that it is not to Leontes but to her daughter that Hermione speaks, calling on the gods to 'pour your graces / Upon my daughter's head'? Although what we see on stage indicates her forgiveness of Leontes – she 'embraces him' and 'hangs about his neck' – her speech is reserved for that which was lost and has been found, the hope that sustained Hermione through the years. Greene's story ends with the suicide of the guilt-ridden Pandosto, but Shakespeare does not take his audience in that direction, explained by Greene disarmingly as a device 'to close up the comedy with a tragical stratagem'. In the final moments of *The Winter's Tale* we are to 'awake our faith' once again, this time in the restoration of happiness to the 'precious winners'. Nevertheless, as so often in Shakespeare's plays, the effect is qualified: Mamillius and Antigonus are both dead, and it is hard not to recall the child's words as he began to tell the bedtime story he never finished: 'A sad tale's best for winter.'

This production of *The Winter's Tale* was first performed as part of the Kenneth Branagh Theatre Company's Plays at the Garrick season, at the Garrick Theatre, London, on 7 November 2015 (previews from 17 October), with the following cast:

MAMILLIUS	Pierre Atri / Rudi Goodman
ARCHIDAMUS	Jaygann Ayeh
FLORIZEL	Tom Bateman
LEONTES	Kenneth Branagh
PERDITA	Jessie Buckley
DORCAS	Vera Chok
CLOWN	Jack Colgrave Hirst
AUTOLYCUS	John Dagleish
PAULINA	Judi Dench
POLIXENES	Hadley Fraser
LORD AMADIS	Adam Garcia
AEGEUM	Matthew Hawksley
CAPNIO	Taylor James
SHEPHERDESS	Pip Jordan
CLEOMENES	Ansu Kabia
DION	Stuart Neal
ANTIGONUS	Michael Pennington
EMILIA	Zoë Rainey
HERMIONE	Miranda Raison
GAOLER	Michael Rouse
CAMILLO	John Shrapnel
MOPSA	Kathryn Wilder
THE SHEPHERD	Jimmy Yuill

Director	Rob Ashford
Director	Kenneth Branagh
Set and Costume Designer	Christopher Oram
Lighting Designer	Neil Austin
Sound Designer	Christopher Shutt
Composer	Patrick Doyle
Projection Designer	Jon Driscoll
Casting Director	Lucy Bevan
Wigs, Hair and Make-up	Carol Hemming
Text Consultant	Russell Jackson
Resident Director	Nicola Samer
Associate Choreographer	Pip Jordan
Voice Consultant	Barbara Houseman
Fight Director	Bret Yount
Set and Costume Design Assistant	Frankie Bradshaw
Casting Associate	Emily Brockmann

PRODUCERS

For The Kenneth Branagh Theatre Company
Kenneth Branagh
Tamar Thomas

For Fiery Angel
Edward Snape
Marilyn Eardley

General Manager for Fiery Angel
Jon Bath

ARTISTIC ASSOCIATES

Rob Ashford
Christopher Oram

COMPANY

Production Manager	Jim Leaver
Costume Supervisor	Mary Charlton
Props Supervisor	Celia Strainge
Wigs Supervisor	Richard Mawbey
Company Manager	Gemma Tonge
Stage Manager	Tanya Gosling
Deputy Stage Managers	Fran O'Donnell
	Rhiannon Harper
Assistant Stage Managers	Stuart Campbell
	Sarah Coates
	Emily Hardy
Head of Wardrobe	Tim Gradwell
Wardrobe Deputy	Rachael Mcintyre
Wardrobe Assistant	Rosie Etheridge
Head of Wigs	Gemma Flaherty
Head of Sound	Wayne Harris
Music Director	Patrick Neil Doyle
Music Supervisor	Maggie Rodford
Music Programmer	Rupert Cross
Lighting Programmer	Rob Halliday
Production Electrician	Martin Chisnall
Production Carpenter	Martin Riley
Dressers	Jenni Carvell
	Spencer Kitchen
Associate Costume Supervisor	Kitty Hawkins
Assistant Props Supervisor	Abby Price
Production Coordinator	Sarah Sweeney
Production Associate	Nick Morrison
Assistant to Kenneth Branagh	Max Gill
Magic and Illusion Consultant	Neil Henry

Kenneth Branagh and Rob Ashford, co-directors
Speaking to Nicola Samer and Max Gill

The Winter's Tale*'s genre is often disputed; how would you classify it?*

RA I think about it as a fairytale. A tale. It is important to always try to remember that. We should worry less about the logic of things, like questioning where Bohemia might be, and more about what it might represent.

KB Dowden grouped *Cymbeline*, *Pericles*, *The Tempest* and *The Winter's Tale* together as 'romances'. A 'romance' in this context works for me because it implies a heightened fable-like quality. I don't think of it as a 'problem play' in the same way as people do of works like *Measure for Measure* or *Troilus and Cressida*. The power of the story has a very deep appeal and although some people might say that it's not realistic, or logical, it is romantic.

Is there a line or image that you think encapsulates the play?

KB Paulina's line 'It is required you do awake your faith'. People at the end of the play may have to do that to receive, understand, or accept miracles. They also may need to do it in order to step closer to forgiveness, or redemption, or reconciliation. Faith is under discussion in the play. Leontes' faith in his wife is shaken, others' faith in him is shattered by his behaviour and everybody seems to need or require, as personified by the actions and character of Hermione, some Grace. The notions of Faith and Grace are embedded in the play.

How have you constructed the world of the play from the text?

KB Sicilia, for all its Mediterranean locale, has a frostiness of human temperature. Sicily is cooler and Bohemia has its vivacity, its spring-like, sheep-shearing intensity, vividly bright, green, and full of life. The play seems full of strong clear contrasts amidst dense language. We've tried to follow the big broad strokes of Shakespeare's simplicity, as per the requirements of a fable or fairytale.

How has The Winter's Tale *developed and changed during the rehearsal process? Has anything surprised you? What advice would you give to yourself on the first day of rehearsals?*

KB The play leans less heavily than perhaps we imagined on the analysis of kingship, royalty, or hierarchy. It goes quickly to a much more personal and universal account of jealousy and the havoc it can wreak. Although there is formal structure and the story of two kingdoms, and two kings, the personal voyage seems to be the one that uncovers itself, particularly in the way that it leads us to understand how isolation and loneliness are produced by the destructive force of jealousy.

RA Unusually for a Shakespeare play, there are no armies, there are no invasions, there are no fears of invasion. There's no urgency in the play because of those kind of circumstances. I find that very fascinating; it is the emotional journey of these people. It's the road to redemption for these characters that actually motors the plot. It has really informed the world we've put them in as far as how the court behaves, how everyone responds personally to Leontes and his accusations against Hermione.

What would you like the audience to leave with?

RA For those out there who feel hopeless, that there is hope.

KB For those who accept that any one of us can make a mistake, but that not anyone can forgive, here is a story with an interesting, complex problem. It's hard not to feel moved by the end of the play, by what the characters have gone through and indeed what they may hope for. Moved, in part, because Shakespeare doesn't give a complete and easy 'happy ending'. It is complex, it is incomplete. It's compassionate but tender, and tenderised, so I think people may feel many things at the end of such an experience. I'd like to think that hope would be one of those things, but it is a hope borne out of a significant and not always easy experience.

Judi Dench said in our interview with her that she considered Leontes the most challenging role in Shakespeare. How have you negotiated that challenge?

KB When you're playing any significant part in Shakespeare, I think you probably think it's the most difficult part. For the actor inside the work, as always, you try to find your own way through it. Not to judge the character, not to worry about the speed at which the character is suddenly in the grip of a certain kind of emotion. I think it's a fascinating part to play because there are echoes of *King Lear*, echoes of *Othello*, echoes of *Macbeth*, and yet it's fused and compressed in a way that makes it particularly intense and unusual.

RA I think it helps in portraying Leontes well to be fearless as an actor and not afraid to show quite a range of emotion and to be able to have those emotions come in and out at a moment's notice, so it's kind of a jumble. It's like a chaos of emotion in his head and then it keeps switching at points, and that's what we get to see as an audience.

The season has an emphasis on the importance of company, why is this important to you both – and why now?

KB When you do several plays together, I think there is a particular interchange of ideas and support. There's a dialogue between more and less experienced people. You seem to have more hands on deck to do the work. You have more examples and inspirations of how the work might be achieved technically, or how difficult language might be spoken naturally. There is a passing of that knowledge around. There's a sense of event.

There's a sense of collaboration that's different from performing a one-off play. There's a kind of transparency about how things are done. When the goal is the pursuit of excellence and you are working on the plays of very fine writers, a high level of skill needs to be acquired and that seems to benefit from being gathered in a specialist group.

RA I also think that when doing three plays at once, there's a triple commitment to working together and creating together.

This season marks the reunion of your artistic collaboration. How do you negotiate this creative relationship?

KB We talk as often as possible. And as early as possible.

RA I would say to obviously make sure that we're both on the same page.

KB Early exchange of information. When we have an idea we share it in person, with a phone call, via email. And sometimes years ahead. First conversations are had as soon as we read the play. We're often creatures of instinct. We try to keep as many positive question marks going as we can.

How have you edited the full text of the play for your production?

KB You end up editing the play in the way that seems to speak to your own experience of the work. This is not a full-length text. The editing and minimal rearrangement of the text is, however, based on an understanding that this is a play that has been robustly moved around before. David Garrick, the man who gave his name to our theatre, is one who famously amended it. I hope we stay on the right side of respecting the text but that we shape and reveal that which goes with our would-be psychological and humane approach to the text. That keeps the 'chamber music' of the play a little more carefully orchestrated than the big epic strokes or the larger musical arcs. We're a little more contained, a little more intimate, and the cuts and amendments reflect that.

Judi Dench and Michael Pennington,
Paulina and Antigonus
Speaking to Nicola Samer and Max Gill

What is the appeal of The Winter's Tale *to a modern audience?*

JD It's not a play that's performed very often. But I think it can
be very exciting if you come to a play without any previous
knowledge, especially Shakespeare, that's why I'm not telling my
grandson about it. I want him to come and *see* it with fresh eyes.

MP You know what happens at the end of *Romeo and Juliet*, but
maybe not *The Winter's Tale*: it always feels like a new play to a
lot of people. And it veers this way and that, between tragedy
and comedy. Anyone who's suffered sexual jealousy, or whose
family has been damaged by it, is going to be caught by the first
half of the play. And then in the second half the power of young
love makes everything possible again: there's a second chance.

JD And some magic if you're lucky.

MP Yes, miracles do happen.

Is there a line in the play that has a particular poignancy for you?

MP The play is dotted with lines you can't forget. When Paulina
says at the end, 'It is required you do awake your faith', it's
almost as if she's giving the play a headline. You have to
believe in the extraordinary thing she's about to do, you have to
suspend your common sense.

When, just before that, Leontes says to Florizel and Perdita,
'Welcome hither, as is the spring to the earth', that's very much
the story of the play too. The second half in Bohemia is entirely
to do with spring coming out of winter, rebirth, fertility, and life
starting again. Redemption in fact.

JD They are such a sharp contrast to the despair of Leontes'
court. Suddenly everybody merrymaking, innocent and with the
whole of life seemingly before them.

What, in your opinion, should we feel at the end of the play?

MP A sort of guarded joy, if there is such a thing. The play is so
nearly a terrible tragedy on the scale of *Othello*. It's as if
Shakespeare wrote *Othello* again in Leontes' raging jealousy
and destructiveness in the first half, and then decided to flip the
play over in the second: at this stage he was certainly more
interested in salvation than tragedy. But you can't forget that
first hour and a half, when people's lives were in danger and
there were real casualties. If you look back through the sunlight
of the second half in Bohemia you can still see the horrors of
the first in Sicilia.

JD I think what one should be left with is the whole arc from
Leontes' blinding jealously at the beginning, through the death
and seeming loss of his whole family and to forgiveness and
reconciliation at the end.

MP It's very hard work. The first three scenes for Leontes are
one frantic burn: it's full throttle but a brilliant study in self-
punishment.

The Winter's Tale *has a particular focus on the passage of Time
and the change it brings. Has your perception of the play
changed since you played Hermione and Perdita for the RSC in
1969; and, Michael, when you played Leontes in 1990?*

JD As I was so busy playing Hermione and Perdita, I didn't
have time to take notice of Brenda Bruce who was simply
wonderful as Paulina, and now I wish I had. It's as if the play
has swivelled around me and I see it from a different angle.
We've had a very good time rehearsing it.

MP I played Leontes when I was about the right age and I loved
his complexity. And this is a favourite play. I've had the good

fortune in my life to play most of Shakespeare's thousand-line parts, and now I've the pleasure of picking out the ones like Antigonus in *The Winter's Tale*, which are more like perfect cameos.

JD A 'bear' cameo!

MP There are parts in Shakespeare, like Mercutio in *Romeo and Juliet*, John of Gaunt in *Richard II*, and now this, that finish early but contain hidden treasures. I'd forgotten how gorgeously written the scene with Antigonus and the baby is, even by Shakespeare's standards, he's at the absolute height of his powers. Wherever you go with this writer, early or late, big parts or smaller, you come across things that are quite extraordinary. It's not that Shakespeare started quite good, and then got better, and then became a genius, he was a genius from the first day.

This production marks a reunion for you both on stage, with Kenneth Branagh and each other. How have these relationships informed your approach to the production?

JD This is the ninth time I've worked with Ken. I love being directed by him and I love acting with him. Having directed him in *Much Ado About Nothing*, I went to Brighton to see how they were getting on. Ken left the theatre in his costume before I could get around to give him notes. I've never let him forget it.

MP This is the fourth time I've been married to Judi Dench. In thirty-seven years. We're serial. I've admired Ken for years and there was a little period in the 1980s, when he had his Renaissance Company and I had the English Shakespeare Company, when we'd occasionally bump into each other criss-crossing the country – in late-night curry houses usually. But we hadn't worked together, and so I was delighted when this came up.

You both have experience as actors and directors. How do you approach a play differently in each respective role?

JD When directing, you have to have an overall view of everything. It's very much a question of orchestration. If you're an actor in a company, you feel like a piece of a jigsaw puzzle, which I must say I enjoy more than having to put it all together myself.

MP They are quite different crafts that on the face of it require quite different skills. I never really enjoyed being the fellow who had to have all the answers: I really prefer to play in the yard with the other kids. It is undoubtedly a very lonely job to be a director: it can be very satisfying but one shouldn't automatically assume that an actor can direct any more than you should assume that a director can act. In acting, you are generally totally absorbed in the dynamics of your own character, while the director is absorbed in all of them. But Ken has the knack of doing both.

What advice do you have for a budding actor in approaching Shakespeare's language?

JD I have always maintained that there are two people who can teach you about speaking Shakespeare; listen to John Gielgud and listen to Frank Sinatra. Gielgud never rested so long on a line that you lost the thread of what went before. Sinatra starts a song and never spends too much time on one particular piece of it. I would also advise anyone to see as much as you can, decide what works for you or what you think doesn't work. Our job is to tell the story to a group of people on a particular night. The next night it will be a different group of people. We'll tell the same story, but it will be to another audience and so the play slightly shifts a little bit each performance.

MP There's one practical thing that everyone should know who's starting out on Shakespeare. We talk in soundbites nowadays, in three- or four-line phrases. But Shakespeare often takes six lines to come to the point. Hamlet asks, 'To be, or not to be, that is the question: / Whether 'tis nobler in the mind to suffer / The slings and arrows of outrageous fortune / Or to take arms against a sea of troubles / And by opposing end them.' But until you get to 'end them', you don't know what point he's making. The danger can be to stop in the middle of a line or dwell on some particularly striking phrase so that you suddenly lose the sense of the whole. There are a lot of schools of thought about how to do Shakespearean verse: 'you should breathe here', 'you shouldn't breathe there'. It becomes almost like a version of opera. The thing to remember is that it is yours. It belongs to you the moment you start doing it. Shakespeare wrote in a language that was understood by intellectuals and by people who could barely read and everyone in between. He found a way of making what he had to say available to absolutely everyone at the same moment. There shouldn't be a mystique to it. Don't be overawed. It is not beyond anyone's gift.

JD Don't underestimate the audience's ability to catch on very quickly.

MP If they're interested.

JD If you're lucky.

Patrick Doyle, composer
Speaking to Nick Morrison

What kind of research did you do before composing the music for The Winter's Tale*?*

Before composing the music for *The Winter's Tale* I listened to a lot of music from Bohemia, indigenous folk music and lots of Czech music, I also researched instruments that still prevail. I was already familiar with music from that part of the world, especially in a classical sense, Dvořák was heavily influenced by indigenous folk music. Writing songs using Shakespeare's words is something I particularly enjoy and something I've been doing for many years with Sir Kenneth Branagh.

Do you start in front of a piano? Tell me a bit about your process. Do you find being in the rehearsal room with the actors influences how your compositions develop?

I invariably write at the piano and when writing songs, clearly, the meter and rhythm of the words are key to the melody and harmony. There are two songs sung by the character Autolycus in *The Winter's Tale*, 'Come Buy' and 'When Daffodils Begin to Peer', I wrote these before rehearsals even began, along with a Sicilian theme, titled 'Tomorrow as Today', which I wrote to capture the world of the court up until we reach Act Four.

Polixenes is the character, who, whilst speaking to Leontes at one point during his speech says 'tomorrow as today'. Ken suggested I set music to a section of this speech and this became a four-part harmony Christmas song sung by the entire cast. A part of this speech was also used in the shepherd and shepherdesses dance in Act Four, sung by Perdita and the actors who also played instruments. The theme from the court,

'Tomorrow as Today', was conceived before rehearsals began and I then adapted the theme to the words of Polixenes' speech.

A great many of Shakespeare's plays feature songs and music – what are the functions that music performs in this production?

The music has various functions: it creates atmosphere and a sense of place, taking the audience through the scene transitions and providing pure entertainment. I began discussing in detail the dances in Act Four long before rehearsals began and there are two dances within the play, 'The Shepherd's Partners Dance' and 'The Reel', a dance by the shepherds and shepherdesses in Act Four. The dances help to reveal the contrast from the court to the relaxed and earthy country life.

What's unique about this production for me is that so many of the actors are also musicians and dancers and they were cast with that in mind. I find that the songs enrich the characterisations of the actors who sing them.

How do you find setting Shakespeare's words to music?

I find Shakespeare's words most inspiring. I very often write songs that, although not originally conceived as such, often form soliloquies and prose.

You have written for many different media and genres in the past. Is there something special about composing for the stage?

I haven't found any great difference between writing for the stage and other media genres. I've written music for songs, musicals, dance and for dramatic underscore, and each demands a sense of drama and lyricism. I encompass all aspects of music and dance in all of my compositions across all genres and media.

You have a history of working with Sir Kenneth Branagh on a variety of projects. What is your working relationship like?

Ken and I have worked alongside each other for over thirty years and we very often read each other's minds. There's a shorthand that develops between two people after working together for such a long time that I find helps to speed the process along and takes away some of the pressure. Ken has always given me lots of artistic musical freedom to compose, the clarity of his ideas gives me a very strong direction and at the same time a great deal of musical space. This always results in a very clear concept each time we embark on a project.

Tomorrow As Today

Sung by The Company

Music by Patrick Doyle

Soprano: We were as twin lambs that did frisk i' th' - sun.

Alto: We were as twin lambs that did frisk i' th' -

Soprano: What we changed was i - nno - cence, For i - nno - cence.

Alto: sun, we changed was i - nno - cence, For i - nno - cence.

Tenor: What we changed was i - nno - cence, For. i - nno - cence.

Bass: What we changed i - nno - cence, For i - nno - cence.

Soprano: But such a day, to - mor - row as to - day.

Alto: But such day, to - mor - row as day. to - day

Tenor: But such but such a day to - day.

Bass: But such day, to - mor - row as day.

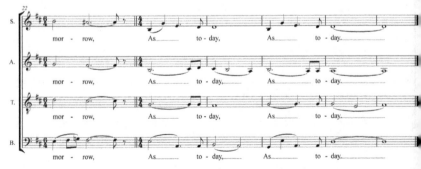

Published by Patrick Doyle Music, Administered by Air-Edel Associates Ltd.

When Daffodils Begin To Peer

Sung by Autolycus

Music by Patrick Doyle

Published by Patrick Doyle Music, Administered by Air-Edel Associates Ltd.

Come Buy

Sung by Autolycus

Music by Patrick Doyle

Lawn as white as dri - ven snow,

Cy - press black as e'er was crow, Gloves as sweet as da - mas - k ro - ses,

Masks for fa - ces and for no - ses,

Bu - gle bra - celet, ne - cklace am - ber, Per - fume for a la - dy's cha - mber,

Gol - den coifs and sto - mach - ers For my lads to give their dears,

Pins and po - king - sticks of steel;

What maids lack from head to heel Come buy of me, come, come buy, come buy;

Buy, lads or else your las - ses cry; Buy, lads or else your las - ses cry; Come, come buy

Published by Patrick Doyle Music, Administered by Air-Edel Associates Ltd.

THE WINTER'S TALE

William Shakespeare

edited by Kenneth Branagh

A Note on the Text
Kenneth Branagh

This version of *The Winter's Tale* is based upon the First Folio and modern scholarship. It has been amended for our production in the following ways:

We have made cuts throughout the play that amount to approximately 600 lines.

We open with a scene between Paulina and Mamillius that usually occurs between Hermione and Mamillius in Act Two Scene One.

We have given the names Amadis, Capnio and Aegeum to Leontes' lords and servants. These names were inspired by characters popular in the literature of Shakespeare's time, including Greene's *Pandosto*.

In Act Two Scene One we have included a moment of dialogue in Russian between Hermione and Mamillius to reflect Hermione's Russian heritage ('The Emperor of Russia was my father', Act Three Scene Two).

We have rearranged the scene order of Act Four, so that Act Four Scene Three precedes Act Four Scene Two.

In Act Four, the role of Servant is taken by the character of Archidamus.

In Act Five Scene Two, the roles of First Gentleman, Second Gentleman, and Third Gentleman are taken by Dion, Cleomenes and Amadis, respectively.

4

Characters

PAULINA
MAMILLIUS
ARCHIDAMUS
CAMILLO
LEONTES
HERMIONE
POLIXENES
FIRST LADY
SECOND LADY
ANTIGONUS
AMADIS
CAPNIO
GAOLER
EMILIA
AEGEUM
CLEOMENES
DION
MARINER
SHEPHERD
CLOWN
AUTOLYCUS
FLORIZEL
PERDITA
MOPSA
DORCAS

And ATTENDANTS, LORDS, LADIES, OFFICERS,
SHEPHERDS

*This text went to press before the end of rehearsals and so may
differ slightly from the play as performed.*

Prologue

Grand Hall in Leontes' Palace. Sicilia.

PAULINA.
Come sir now. Pray sit you by us
And tell's a tale.

MAMILLIUS.
Merry or sad shalt be?

PAULINA.
As merry as you will.

MAMILLIUS.
A sad tale's best for winter. I have one
Of sprites and goblins.

PAULINA.
Let's have that good sir.

Music – carol: 'Deck the Halls'.

COMPANY.
Deck the halls with boughs of holly,
Fa la, la, la, la, la, la, la, la
'Tis the season to be jolly,
Fa la, la, la, la, la, la, la, la

Don we now our gay apparel,
Fa la, la, la, la, la, la, la, la
Troll the ancient yuletide carol,
Fa la, la, la, la, la, la, la, la

See the blazing yule before us,
Fa la, la, la, la, la, la, la, la
Strike the harp and join the chorus,
Fa la, la, la, la, la, la, la, la

Follow me in merry measure,
Fa la, la, la, la, la, la, la, la
While I tell of yuletide treasure,
Fa la, la, la, la, la, la, la, la.

ACT ONE

Scene One

Grand Hall in Leontes' Palace. Sicilia.

Enter CAMILLO *and* ARCHIDAMUS.

ARCHIDAMUS.
If you shall chance, Camillo, to visit Bohemia, on the like occasion whereon my services are now on foot, you shall see, as I have said, great difference betwixt our Bohemia and your Sicilia.

CAMILLO.
I think, this coming summer, the King of Sicilia means to pay Bohemia the visitation which he justly owes him.

ARCHIDAMUS.
Wherein our entertainment shall shame us we will be justified in our loves; for indeed –

CAMILLO.
Beseech you, –

ARCHIDAMUS.
Verily, I speak it in the freedom of my knowledge: we cannot with such magnificence – in so rare – I know not what to say. We will give you sleepy drinks, that your senses, unintelligent of our insufficience, may, though they cannot praise us, as little accuse us.

CAMILLO.
You pay a great deal too dear for what's given freely.

ARCHIDAMUS.
Believe me, I speak as my understanding instructs me and as mine honesty puts it to utterance.

CAMILLO.
Sicilia cannot show himself over-kind to Bohemia. They were trained together in their childhoods; and there rooted

betwixt them then such an affection, which cannot choose
but branch now. Since their more mature dignities and royal
necessities made separation of their society, their encounters,
though not personal, have been royally attorneyed with
interchange of gifts, letters, loving embassies; that they have
seemed to be together, though absent, shook hands, as over a
vast, and embraced, as it were, from the ends of opposed
winds. The heavens continue their loves!

ARCHIDAMUS.

I think there is not in the world either malice or matter to
alter it. You have an unspeakable comfort of your young
Prince Mamillius: it is a gentleman of the greatest promise
that ever came into my note.

CAMILLO.

I very well agree with you in the hopes of him: it is a gallant
child; one that indeed physics the subject, makes old hearts
fresh: they that went on crutches ere he was born desire yet
their life to see him a man.

ARCHIDAMUS.

Would they else be content to die?

CAMILLO.

Yes; if there were no other excuse why they should
desire to live.

ARCHIDAMUS.

If the king had no son, they would desire to live
on crutches till he had one.

Enter LEONTES, HERMIONE, MAMILLIUS,
POLIXENES, CAMILLO, *and* ATTENDANTS.

POLIXENES.

Nine changes of the watery star hath been
The shepherd's note since we have left our throne
Without a burden: time as long again
Would be filled up, my brother, with our thanks;
And yet we should, for perpetuity,
Go hence in debt: and therefore, like a cipher,
Yet standing in rich place, I multiply
With one 'We thank you' many thousands moe
That go before it.

LEONTES.
                    Stay your thanks a while;
    And pay them when you part.

POLIXENES.
                         Sir, that's tomorrow.
    I am question'd by my fears, of what may chance
    Or breed upon our absence; that may blow
    No sneaping winds at home, to make us say
    'This is put forth too truly': besides, I have stay'd
    To tire your royalty.

LEONTES.
                    We are tougher, brother,
    Than you can put us to't.

POLIXENES.
                         No longer stay.

LEONTES.
    One seven-night longer.

POLIXENES.
                    Very sooth, tomorrow.

LEONTES.
    We'll part the time between's then; and in that
    I'll no gainsaying.

POLIXENES.
                    Press me not, beseech you, so.
    There is no tongue that moves, none, none i' the world,
    So soon as yours could win me: my affairs
    Do even drag me homeward: which to hinder
    Were in your love a whip to me; my stay
    To you a charge and trouble: to save both,
    Farewell, our brother.

LEONTES.
                    Tongue-tied, our queen? speak you.

HERMIONE.
    I had thought, sir, to have held my peace until
    You have drawn oaths from him not to stay. You, sir,
    Charge him too coldly. Tell him, you are sure

All in Bohemia's well; this satisfaction
The by-gone day proclaim'd: say this to him,
He's beat from his best ward.

LEONTES.

Well said, Hermione.

HERMIONE.

To tell, he longs to see his son, were strong:
But let him say so then, and let him go;
But let him swear so, and he shall not stay,
We'll thwack him hence with distaffs.
Yet of your royal presence I'll adventure
The borrow of a week. When at Bohemia
You take my lord, I'll give him my commission
To let him there a month behind the date
Prefix'd for's parting: yet, indeed, Leontes,
I love thee not a jar o' the clock behind
What lady-she her lord. You'll stay?

POLIXENES.

No, madam.

HERMIONE.

Nay, but you will?

POLIXENES.

I may not, verily.

HERMIONE.

Verily!
You put me off with limber vows; but I,
Though you would seek to unsphere the stars with oaths,
Should yet say 'Sir, no going.' Verily,
You shall not go: a lady's 'Verily' 's
As potent as a lord's. Will you go yet?
Force me to keep you as a prisoner,
Not like a guest; so you shall pay your fees
When you depart, and save your thanks. How say you?
My prisoner? or my guest? by your dread 'Verily',
One of them you shall be.

POLIXENES.

Your guest, then, madam:
To be your prisoner should import offending;

Which is for me less easy to commit
Than you to punish.

HERMIONE.

Not your gaoler, then,
But your kind hostess. Come, I'll question you
Of my lord's tricks and yours when you were boys:
You were pretty lordings then?

POLIXENES.

We were, fair queen,
Two lads that thought there was no more behind
But such a day tomorrow as today,
And to be boy eternal.

HERMIONE.

Was not my lord
The verier wag o' the two?

POLIXENES.

We were as twinn'd lambs that did frisk i' the sun,
And bleat the one at the other: what we changed
Was innocence for innocence; we knew not
The doctrine of ill-doing, nor dream'd
That any did. Had we pursued that life,
And our weak spirits ne'er been higher rear'd
With stronger blood, we should have answer'd heaven
Boldly 'not guilty'; the imposition clear'd
Hereditary ours.

HERMIONE.

By this we gather
You have tripp'd since.

POLIXENES.

O my most sacred lady!
Temptations have since then been born to's; for
In those unfledged days was my wife a girl;
Your precious self had then not cross'd the eyes
Of my young play-fellow.

HERMIONE.

Grace to boot!
Of this make no conclusion, lest you say
Your queen and I are devils: yet go on;

The offences we have made you do we'll answer,
If you first sinn'd with us and that with us
You did continue fault and that you slipp'd not
With any but with us.

LEONTES.

Is he won yet?

HERMIONE.
He'll stay my lord.

LEONTES.

At my request he would not.
Hermione, my dearest, thou never spokest
To better purpose.

HERMIONE.

Never?

LEONTES.

Never, but once.

HERMIONE.
What! have I twice said well? when was't before?
Nay, let me have't; I long.

LEONTES.

Why, that was when
Three crabbed months had sour'd themselves to death,
Ere I could make thee open thy white hand
And clap thyself my love: then didst thou utter
'I am yours forever'.

HERMIONE.

'Tis grace indeed.
Why, lo you now, I have spoke to the purpose twice:
The one for ever earn'd a royal husband;
The other for some while a friend.

Giving her hand to POLIXENES.

Music – carol: 'Tomorrow as Today' underscores ice-skating and speech.

COMPANY.
We were as twin lambs, that did frisk i' th' sun
What we changed was innocence, for innocence

But such a day, tomorrow as today.
And to be, and to be, boy eternal.

Two lads that thought there was no more.
But such a day, tomorrow as today
As today, day.

LEONTES.
(*Aside.*)   Too hot, too hot!
To mingle friendship far is mingling bloods.
I have tremor cordis on me: my heart dances;
But not for joy; not joy. This entertainment
May a free face put on, derive a liberty
From heartiness, from bounty, fertile bosom,
And well become the agent; 't may, I grant;
But to be paddling palms and pinching fingers,
As now they are, and making practised smiles,
As in a looking-glass, and then to sigh, as 'twere
The mort o' the deer; O, that is entertainment
My bosom likes not, nor my brows! Mamillius,
Art thou my boy?

MAMILLIUS.
                    Ay, my good lord.

LEONTES.
                              I' faith!
Why, that's my bawcock. What, hast smutch'd thy nose?
They say it is a copy out of mine. Come, captain,
We must be neat; not neat, but cleanly, captain:
And yet the steer, the heifer and the calf
Are all call'd neat. – Still virginalling
Upon his palm! – How now, you wanton calf!
Art thou my calf?

MAMILLIUS.
                    Yes, if you will, my lord.

LEONTES.
Thou want'st a rough pash and the shoots that I have,
To be full like me: yet they say we are
Almost as like as eggs; women say so,
That will say anything, yet it were true

To say this boy were like me. Come, sir page,
Look on me with your welkin eye: sweet villain!
Most dear'st! my collop! Can thy dam? – may't be? –
Affection! thy intention stabs the centre:
Thou dost make possible things not so held,
Communicatest with dreams; – how can this be? –

POLIXENES.
What means Sicilia?

HERMIONE.
He something seems unsettled.

POLIXENES.
How, my lord!
What cheer? how is't with you, best brother?

HERMIONE.
You look as if you held a brow of much distraction
Are you moved, my lord?

LEONTES.
Looking on the lines of my boy's face, methoughts I did recoil
Some many years, and saw myself unbreech'd,
In my green velvet coat, my dagger muzzled,
Lest it should bite its master, and so prove,
As ornaments oft do, too dangerous:
Mine honest friend,
Will you take eggs for money?

MAMILLIUS.
No, my lord, I'll fight.

LEONTES.
You will! why, happy man be's dole! My brother,
Are you so fond of your young prince as we
Do seem to be of ours?

POLIXENES.
If at home, sir,
He's all my exercise, my mirth, my matter,
Now my sworn friend and then mine enemy,
My parasite, my soldier, statesman, all:
He makes a July's day short as December,

And with his varying childness cures in me
Thoughts that would thick my blood.

LEONTES.
                                        So stands this squire
Officed with me: we two will walk, my lord,
And leave you to your graver steps. Hermione,
How thou lovest us, show in our brother's welcome;
Let what is dear in Sicily be cheap:
Next to thyself and my young rover, he's
Apparent to my heart.

HERMIONE.
                        If you would seek us,
We are yours i' the garden: shall's attend you there?

LEONTES.
To your own bents dispose you: you'll be found,
Be you beneath the sky. (*Aside*.) I am angling now,
Though you perceive me not how I give line.
Go to, go to!
How she holds up the neb, the bill to him!
And arms her with the boldness of a wife
To her allowing husband!

Exeunt POLIXENES, HERMIONE, *and* ATTENDANTS.

                        Gone already!
Inch-thick, knee-deep, o'er head and ears a fork'd one?
Go, play, boy, play: thy mother plays, and I
Play too, but so disgraced a part, whose issue
Will hiss me to my grave: contempt and clamour
Will be my knell. Go, play, boy, play. There have been,
Or I am much deceived, cuckolds ere now;
And many a man there is, even at this present,
Now while I speak this, holds his wife by the arm,
That little thinks she has been sluiced in's absence
And his pond fish'd by his next neighbour, by
Sir Smile, his neighbour: nay, there's comfort in't
Whiles other men have gates and those gates open'd,
As mine, against their will. Should all despair
That have revolted wives, the tenth of mankind
Would hang themselves. Physic for't there is none;

It is a bawdy planet, that will strike
Where 'tis predominant; and 'tis powerful, think it,
From east, west, north and south: be it concluded,
No barricado for a belly; know't;
It will let in and out the enemy
With bag and baggage: many thousand on's
Have the disease, and feel't not. How now, boy!

MAMILLIUS.
I am like you, they say.

LEONTES.
                    Why that's some comfort.
What, Camillo there?

CAMILLO.
                    Ay, my good lord.

LEONTES.
Go play, Mamillius; thou'rt an honest man.

Exit MAMILLIUS.

Camillo, this great sir will yet stay longer.

CAMILLO.
You had much ado to make his anchor hold:
When you cast out, it still came home.

LEONTES.
                              Didst note it?

CAMILLO.
He would not stay at your petitions: made
His business more material.

LEONTES.
                    Didst perceive it?
(*Aside*.) They're here with me already, whispering, rounding
'Sicilia is a so-forth': 'tis far gone,
When I shall gust it last. How came't, Camillo,
That he did stay?

CAMILLO.
                    At the good queen's entreaty.

LEONTES.
At the queen's be't: 'good' should be pertinent
But, so it is, it is not. Was this taken
By any understanding pate but thine?

CAMILLO.
My lord! I think most understand
Bohemia stays here longer.

LEONTES.
                              Ha!

CAMILLO.
                              Stays here longer.

LEONTES.
Ay, but why?

CAMILLO.
To satisfy your highness and the entreaties
Of our most gracious mistress.

LEONTES.
                              Satisfy!
The entreaties of your mistress! satisfy!
Let that suffice. I have trusted thee, Camillo,
With all the nearest things to my heart, as well
My chamber-councils, wherein, priest-like, thou
Hast cleansed my bosom, I from thee departed
Thy penitent reform'd: but we have been
Deceived in thy integrity, deceived
In that which seems so.

CAMILLO.
                              Be it forbid, my lord!

LEONTES.
To bide upon't, thou art not honest, or,
If thou inclinest that way, thou art a coward,
Or else thou must be counted
A servant grafted in my serious trust
And therein negligent; or else a fool
That seest a game play'd home, the rich stake drawn,
And takest it all for jest.

CAMILLO.

My gracious lord,
I may be negligent, foolish and fearful;
In every one of these no man is free,
But that his negligence, his folly, fear,
Among the infinite doings of the world,
Sometime puts forth. In your affairs, my lord,
If ever I were wilful-negligent,
It was my folly; if industriously
I play'd the fool, it was my negligence,
Not weighing well the end; if ever fearful
To do a thing, where I the issue doubted,
Where of the execution did cry out
Against the non-performance, 'twas a fear
Which oft infects the wisest: these, my lord,
Are such allow'd infirmities that honesty
Is never free of. But beseech your grace,
Be plainer with me.

LEONTES.

Ha' not you seen, Camillo, –
But that's past doubt, you have, or your eye-glass
Is thicker than a cuckold's horn, – or heard, –
For to a vision so apparent rumour
Cannot be mute, – or thought, – for cogitation
Resides not in that man that does not think, –
My wife is slippery? If thou wilt confess,
Or else be impudently negative,
To have nor eyes nor ears nor thought, then say
My wife's a hobby-horse, deserves a name
As rank as any flax-wench that puts to
Before her troth-plight: say't and justify't.

CAMILLO.

I would not be a stander-by to hear
My sovereign mistress clouded so, without
My present vengeance taken: 'shrew my heart,
You never spoke what did become you less
Than this; which to reiterate were sin
As deep as that, though true.

LEONTES.
                              Is whispering nothing?
Is leaning cheek to cheek? is meeting noses?
Kissing with inside lip? stopping the career
Of laughter with a sigh? – a note infallible
Of breaking honesty – horsing foot on foot?
Skulking in corners? wishing clocks more swift?
Hours, minutes? noon, midnight? and all eyes
Blind with the pin and web but theirs, theirs only,
That would unseen be wicked? is this nothing?
Why, then the world and all that's in't is nothing;
The covering sky is nothing; Bohemia nothing;
My wife is nothing; nor nothing have these nothings,
If this be nothing.

CAMILLO.
                        Good my lord, be cured
Of this diseased opinion, and betimes;
For 'tis most dangerous.

LEONTES.
                              Say it be, 'tis true.

CAMILLO.
    No, no, my lord.

LEONTES.
                              It is; you lie, you lie:
I say thou liest, Camillo, and I hate thee,
Pronounce thee a gross lout, a mindless slave,
Or else a hovering temporiser, that
Canst with thine eyes at once see good and evil,
Inclining to them both: were my wife's liver
Infected as her life, she would not live
The running of one glass.

CAMILLO.
                              Who does infect her?

LEONTES.
    Why, he that wears her like her medal, hanging
About his neck, Bohemia: who, if I
Had servants true about me, they'd do that
Which should undo more doing: ay, and thou,

His cupbearer, – whom I from meaner form
Have benched and reared to worship, who mayst see
Plainly as heaven sees earth and earth sees heaven,
How I am galled, – mightst bespice a cup,
To give mine enemy a lasting wink;
Which draught to me were cordial.

CAMILLO.
                                    Sir, my lord,
I could do this, and that with no rash potion,
But with a lingering dram that should not work
Maliciously like poison: but I cannot
Believe this crack to be in my dread mistress,
So sovereignly being honourable.
I have loved thee, –

LEONTES.
Make that thy question, and go rot!
Dost think I am so muddy, so unsettled,
To appoint myself in this vexation, sully
The purity and whiteness of my sheets,
Which to preserve is sleep, which being spotted
Is goads, thorns, nettles, tails of wasps,
Give scandal to the blood o' the prince my son,
Who I do think is mine and love as mine,
Without ripe moving to't? Would I do this?
Could man so blench?

CAMILLO.
                                    I must believe you, sir:
I do; and will fetch off Bohemia for't;
Provided that, when he's removed, your highness
Will take again your queen as yours at first,
Even for your son's sake.

LEONTES.
                                    Thou dost advise me
Even so as I mine own course have set down:
I'll give no blemish to her honour, none.

CAMILLO.
My lord,
Go then; and with a countenance as clear

As friendship wears at feasts, keep with Bohemia
And with your queen. I am his cupbearer:
If from me he have wholesome beverage,
Account me not your servant.

LEONTES.
                              This is all:
Do't and thou hast the one half of my heart;
Do't not, thou split'st thine own.

CAMILLO.
I'll do't, my lord.

LEONTES.
I will seem friendly, as thou hast advised me.

Exit.

CAMILLO.
O miserable lady! But, for me,
What case stand I in? I must be the poisoner
Of good Polixenes; and my ground to do't
Is the obedience to a master, one
Who in rebellion with himself will have
All that are his so too. To do this deed,
Promotion follows. If I could find example
Of thousands that had struck anointed kings
And flourish'd after, I'ld not do't; but since
Nor brass nor stone nor parchment bears not one,
Let villany itself forswear't. I must
Forsake the court: to do't, or no, is certain
To me a break-neck. Happy star, reign now!
Here comes Bohemia.

Re-enter POLIXENES.

POLIXENES.
                         This is strange: methinks
My favour here begins to warp. Not speak?
Good day, Camillo.

CAMILLO.
                         Hail, most royal sir!

POLIXENES.
  What is the news i' the court?

CAMILLO.
                              None rare, my lord.

POLIXENES.
  The king hath on him such a countenance
  As he had lost some province and a region
  Loved as he loves himself: even now I met him
  With customary compliment; when he,
  Wafting his eyes to the contrary and falling
  A lip of much contempt, speeds from me and
  So leaves me to consider what is breeding
  That changeth thus his manners.

CAMILLO.
                              I dare not know, my lord.

POLIXENES.
  How! dare not! do not. Do you know, and dare not?
  Be intelligent to me: Good Camillo,
  Your changed complexions are to me a mirror
  Which shows me mine changed too; for I must be
  A party in this alteration, finding
  Myself thus alter'd with 't.

CAMILLO.
                              There is a sickness
  Which puts some of us in distemper, but
  I cannot name the disease; and it is caught
  Of you that yet are well.

POLIXENES.
                              How! caught of me!
  Make me not sighted like the basilisk:
  I have look'd on thousands, who have sped the better
  By my regard, but kill'd none so. Camillo, –
  As you are certainly a gentleman, I beseech you,
  If you know aught which does behove my knowledge
  Thereof to be inform'd, imprison't not
  In ignorant concealment.

CAMILLO.

I may not answer.

POLIXENES.

A sickness caught of me, and yet I well!
I must be answer'd. Dost thou hear, Camillo,
I conjure thee, by all the parts of man
Which honour does acknowledge, whereof the least
Is not this suit of mine, that thou declare
What incidency thou dost guess of harm
Is creeping toward me; how far off, how near;
Which way to be prevented, if to be;
If not, how best to bear it.

CAMILLO.

Sir, I will tell you;
Since I am charged in honour and by him
That I think honourable: therefore mark my counsel,
Which must be even as swiftly follow'd as
I mean to utter it, or both yourself and me
Cry lost, and so good night!

POLIXENES.

On, good Camillo.

CAMILLO.

I am appointed him to murder you.

POLIXENES.

By whom, Camillo?

CAMILLO.

By the king.

POLIXENES.

For what?

CAMILLO.

He thinks, nay, with all confidence he swears,
As he had seen't or been an instrument
To vice you to't, that you have touch'd his queen
Forbiddenly.

POLIXENES.

O, then my best blood turn

To an infected jelly and my name
Be yoked with his that did betray the Best!

CAMILLO.

You may as well
Forbid the sea for to obey the moon
As or by oath remove or counsel shake
The fabric of his folly, whose foundation
Is piled upon his faith.

POLIXENES.

How should this grow?

CAMILLO.

I know not: but I am sure 'tis safer to
Avoid what's grown than question how 'tis born.
If therefore you dare trust my honesty, away tonight!
Your followers I will whisper to the business,
And will by twos and threes at several posterns
Clear them o' the city. For myself, I'll put
My fortunes to your service, which are here
By this discovery lost. Be not uncertain;
For, by the honour of my parents, I
Have utter'd truth: which if you seek to prove,
I dare not stand by; nor shall you be safer
Than one condemn'd by the king's own mouth, thereon
His execution sworn.

POLIXENES.

I do believe thee:
I saw his heart in 's face. Give me thy hand:
Be pilot to me and thy places shall
Still neighbour mine. My ships are ready and
My people did expect my hence departure
Two days ago. This jealousy
Is for a precious creature: as she's rare,
Must it be great, and as his person's mighty,
Must it be violent, and as he does conceive
He is dishonour'd by a man which ever
Profess'd to him, why, his revenges must
In that be made more bitter. Fear o'ershades me:
Good expedition be my friend, and comfort

The gracious queen, part of his theme, but nothing
Of his ill-ta'en suspicion!

CAMILLO.
Please your highness
To take the urgent hour. Come, sir, away.

Exeunt.

ACT TWO

Scene One

A room in Leontes' Palace.

Enter HERMIONE, MAMILLIUS, *and* LADIES.

HERMIONE.
   Kuda, kuda?

MAMILLIUS.
   Mamushka.

HERMIONE.
   Take the boy to you: he so troubles me,
   'Tis past enduring.

FIRST LADY.
               Come, my gracious lord,
   Shall I be your playfellow?

MAMILLIUS.
                 No, I'll none of you.

FIRST LADY.
   Why, my sweet lord?

MAMILLIUS.
   You'll kiss me hard and speak to me as if
   I were a baby still. I love you better.

SECOND LADY.
   And why so, my lord?

MAMILLIUS.
            Not for because
   Your brows are blacker; yet black brows, they say,
   Become some women best, so that there be not
   Too much hair there, but in a semicircle
   Or a half-moon made with a pen.

SECOND LADY.
Who taught you this?

MAMILLIUS.
I learnt it out of women's faces. Pray now
What colour are your eyebrows?

SECOND LADY.
                                        Blue, my lord.

MAMILLIUS.
Nay, that's a mock: I have seen a lady's nose
That has been blue, but not her eyebrows.

FIRST LADY.
                                        Hark ye;
The queen your mother rounds apace: we shall
Present our services to a fine new prince
One of these days; and then you'ld wanton with us,
If we would have you.

SECOND LADY.
                        She is spread of late
Into a goodly bulk: good time encounter her!

HERMIONE.
What wisdom stirs amongst you? Come, sir, now
I am for you again:
Come on, sit down: come on, and do your best
To fright me with your sprites; you're powerful at it.

MAMILLIUS.
There was a man –

HERMIONE.
                        Nay, come, sit down; then on.

MAMILLIUS.
Dwelt by a churchyard: I will tell it softly;
Yond crickets shall not hear it.

HERMIONE.
Come on, then,
And give't me in mine ear.

Enter LEONTES, *with* ANTIGONUS, LORDS *and others.*

LEONTES.

Was he met there? his train? Camillo with him?

AMADIS.

Behind the tuft of pines I met them; never
Saw I men scour so on their way: I eyed them
Even to their ships.

LEONTES.

How blest am I
In my just censure, in my true opinion!
Alack, for lesser knowledge! how accursed
In being so blest! There may be in the cup
A spider steep'd, and one may drink, depart,
And yet partake no venom, for his knowledge
Is not infected: but if one present
The abhorr'd ingredient to his eye, make known
How he hath drunk, he cracks his gorge, his sides,
With violent hefts. I have drunk, and seen the spider.
Camillo was his help in this, his pander:
There is a plot against my life, my crown;
All's true that is mistrusted: How came the posterns
So easily open?

AMADIS.

By his great authority;
Which often hath no less prevail'd than so
On your command.

LEONTES.

I know't too well.
Give me the boy: I am glad you did not nurse him:
Though he does bear some signs of me, yet you
Have too much blood in him.

HERMIONE.

What is this? sport?

LEONTES.

Bear the boy hence; he shall not come about her;
Away with him! and let her sport herself
With that she's big with; for 'tis Polixenes
Has made thee swell thus.

HERMIONE.

But I'ld say he had not,
And I'll be sworn you would believe my saying,
Howe'er you lean to the nayward.

LEONTES.

You, my lords,
Look on her, mark her well; be but about
To say 'she is a goodly lady', and
The justice of your hearts will thereto add
'Tis pity she's not honest, For be 't known,
From him that has most cause to grieve it should be,
She's an adulteress.

HERMIONE.

Should a villain say so,
The most replenish'd villain in the world,
He were as much more villain: you, my lord,
Do but mistake.

LEONTES.

You have mistook, my lady,
Polixenes for Leontes: I have said
She's an adulteress; I have said with whom:
More, she's a traitor and Camillo is
A federary with her, and one that knows
What she should shame to know herself
But with her most vile principal, that she's
A bed-swerver, ay, and privy
To this their late escape.

HERMIONE.

No, by my life.
Privy to none of this. How will this grieve you,
When you shall come to clearer knowledge, that
You thus have publish'd me! Gentle my lord,
You scarce can right me throughly then to say
You did mistake.

LEONTES.

Away with her! to prison!
He who shall speak for her is afar off guilty
But that he speaks.

HERMIONE.
There's some ill planet reigns:
I must be patient till the heavens look
With an aspect more favourable. Good my lords,
I am not prone to weeping, as our sex
Commonly are; the want of which vain dew
Perchance shall dry your pities: but I have
That honourable grief lodged here which burns
Worse than tears drown: beseech you all, my lords,
With thoughts so qualified as your charities
Shall best instruct you, measure me; and so
The king's will be perform'd!

LEONTES.
Shall I be heard?

HERMIONE.
Who is't that goes with me? Beseech your highness,
My women may be with me; for you see
My plight requires it. Do not weep, good fools;
There is no cause: when you shall know your mistress
Has deserved prison, then abound in tears
As I come out: this action I now go on
Is for my better grace. Adieu, my lord:
I never wish'd to see you sorry; now
I trust I shall. My women, come; you have leave.

LEONTES.
Go, do our bidding; hence!

Exit HERMIONE, *guarded; with* LADIES.

AMADIS.
Beseech your highness, call the queen again.

ANTIGONUS.
Be certain what you do, sir, lest your justice
Prove violence; in the which three great ones suffer,
Yourself, your queen, your son.

AMADIS.
For her, my lord,
I dare my life lay down and will do't, sir,
Please you to accept it, that the queen is spotless

I' the eyes of heaven and to you; I mean,
In this which you accuse her.

ANTIGONUS.

               If it prove
She's otherwise, I'll keep my stables where
I lodge my wife; I'll go in couples with her;
Than when I feel and see her no farther trust her;
For every inch of woman in the world,
Ay, every dram of woman's flesh is false,
If she be.

LEONTES.

        Hold your peaces.

AMADIS.

              Good my lord, –

ANTIGONUS.

It is for you we speak, not for ourselves:
You are abused and by some putter-on
That will be damn'd for't; would I knew the villain,
I would land-damn him. Be she honour-flaw'd,
I have three granddaughters; the eldest is eleven
The second and the third, nine, and some five;
If this prove true, they'll pay for't: by mine honour,
I'll geld 'em all; fourteen they shall not see,
To bring false generations: they are co-heirs;
And I had rather geld myself than they
Should not produce fair issue.

LEONTES.

              Cease; no more.
You smell this business with a sense as cold
As is a dead man's nose: but I do see't and feel't
As you feel doing thus; and see withal
The instruments that feel.

ANTIGONUS.

           If it be so,
We need no grave to bury honesty:
There's not a grain of it the face to sweeten
Of the whole dungy earth.

LEONTES.

What! lack I credit?

AMADIS.

I had rather you did lack than I, my lord,
Upon this ground; and more it would content me
To have her honour true than your suspicion,
Be blamed for't how you might.

LEONTES.

Why, what need we
Commune with you of this, but rather follow
Our forceful instigation? Our prerogative
Calls not your counsels, inform yourselves
We need no more of your advice: the matter,
The loss, the gain, the ordering on't, is all
Properly ours.

ANTIGONUS.

And I wish, my liege,
You had only in your silent judgment tried it,
Without more overture.

LEONTES.

How could that be?
Either thou art most ignorant by age,
Or thou wert born a fool. Camillo's flight,
Added to their familiarity,
Which was as gross as ever touch'd conjecture,
That lack'd sight only doth push on this proceeding:
Yet, for a greater confirmation,
For in an act of this importance 'twere
Most piteous to be wild, I have dispatch'd in post
To sacred Delphos, to Apollo's temple,
Cleomenes and Dion, whom you know
Of stuff'd sufficiency: now from the Oracle
They will bring all; whose spiritual counsel had,
Shall stop or spur me. Have I done well?

AMADIS.

Well done, my lord.

LEONTES.

Though I am satisfied and need no more

Than what I know, yet shall the Oracle
Give rest to the minds of others, such as he
Whose ignorant credulity will not
Come up to the truth. So have we thought it good
From our free person she should be confined,
Lest that the treachery of the two fled hence
Be left her to perform. Come, follow us;
We are to speak in public; for this business
Will raise us all.

ANTIGONUS.
(*Aside*.)   To laughter, as I take it,
If the good truth were known.

Exeunt.

Scene Two

A prison.

Enter PAULINA, CAPNIO, *and* LADIES-IN-WAITING.

PAULINA.
The keeper of the prison, call to him;
Let him have knowledge who I am.

Exit CAPNIO.

                              Good lady,
No court in Europe is too good for thee;
What dost thou then in prison?

Re-enter CAPNIO, *with the* GAOLER.

                              Now, good sir,
You know me, do you not?

GAOLER.
                              For a worthy lady
And one whom much I honour.

PAULINA.

                              Pray you then,
Conduct me to the queen.

GAOLER.

                    I may not, madam:
To the contrary I have express commandment.

PAULINA.
Here's ado,
To lock up honesty and honour from
The access of gentle visitors!
Is't lawful, pray you,
To see her women? any of them? Emilia?

GAOLER.
So please you, madam,
To put apart these your attendants, I
Shall bring Emilia forth.

PAULINA.

                    I pray now, call her.
Withdraw yourselves.

    Exeunt LADIES-IN-WAITING.

GAOLER.

                    And, madam,
I must be present at your conference.

PAULINA.
Well, be't so, prithee.

    Exit GAOLER.

Here's such ado to make no stain a stain
As passes colouring.

    Re-enter GAOLER, *with* EMILIA.

                    Dear gentlewoman,
How fares our gracious lady?

EMILIA.
As well as one so great and so forlorn
May hold together: on her frights and griefs,

Which never tender lady hath born greater,
She is something before her time deliver'd.

PAULINA.
A boy?

EMILIA.
A daughter, and a goodly babe,
Lusty and like to live: the queen receives
Much comfort in't; says 'My poor prisoner,
I am innocent as you.'

PAULINA.
I dare be sworn
These dangerous unsafe lunes i' the king, beshrew them!
He must be told on't, and he shall: the office
Becomes a woman best;
Pray you, Emilia, commend my best obedience to the queen:
If she dares trust me with her little babe,
I'll show't the king and undertake to be
Her advocate to the loud'st. We do not know
How he may soften at the sight o' the child:
The silence often of pure innocence
Persuades when speaking fails.

EMILIA.
Most worthy madam,
Your honour and your goodness is so evident
That your free undertaking cannot miss
A thriving issue: there is no lady living
So meet for this great errand. Please your ladyship
To visit the next room, I'll presently
Acquaint the queen of your most noble offer;
Who but today hammer'd of this design,
But durst not tempt a minister of honour,
Lest she should be denied.

PAULINA.
Tell her, Emilia.
I'll use that tongue I have: if wit flow from't
As boldness from my bosom, let 't not be doubted
I shall do good.

EMILIA.
Now be you blest for it!
I'll to the queen: please you, come something nearer.

GAOLER.
Madam, if't please the queen to send the babe,
I know not what I shall incur to pass it,
Having no warrant.

PAULINA.
You need not fear it, sir:
This child was prisoner to the womb and is
By law and process of great nature thence
Freed and enfranchised, not a party to
The anger of the king nor guilty of,
If any be, the trespass of the queen.

GAOLER.
I do believe it.

PAULINA.
Do not you fear: upon mine honour,
I will stand betwixt you and danger.

Exeunt.

Scene Three

A room in Leontes' Palace.

Enter LEONTES.

LEONTES.
Nor night nor day no rest: it is but weakness
To bear the matter thus; mere weakness. If
The cause were not in being, – part o' the cause,
She the adulteress; for the harlot king
Is quite beyond mine arm, out of the blank
And level of my brain, plot-proof; but she
I can hook to me: say that she were gone,

Given to the fire, a moiety of my rest
Might come to me again. Who's there?

Enter AEGEUM.

AEGEUM.

My lord?

LEONTES.
How does the boy?

AEGEUM.
He took good rest tonight;
'Tis hoped his sickness is discharged.

LEONTES.

To see his nobleness!
Conceiving the dishonour of his mother,
He straight declined, droop'd, took it deeply,
Fasten'd and fix'd the shame on't in himself,
Threw off his spirit, his appetite, his sleep,
And downright languish'd. Leave me solely: go,
See how he fares.

Exit AEGEUM.

Camillo and Polixenes
Laugh at me, make their pastime at my sorrow:
They should not laugh if I could reach them, nor
Shall she within my power.

Enter AEGEUM *trying to stop* PAULINA, ANTIGONUS,
CAPNIO, AMADIS, *and* EMILIA *with a child.*

AEGEUM.

You must not enter.

PAULINA.
Nay, rather, good my lords, be second to me:
Fear you his tyrannous passion more, alas,
Than the queen's life? a gracious innocent soul,
More free than he is jealous.

ANTIGONUS.

That's enough.

AEGEUM.

Madam, he hath not slept tonight; commanded
None should come at him.

PAULINA.

Not so hot, good sir:
I come to bring him sleep. 'Tis such as you,
That creep like shadows by him and do sigh
At each his needless heavings, such as you
Nourish the cause of his awaking: I
Do come with words as medicinal as true,
Honest as either, to purge him of that humour
That presses him from sleep.

LEONTES.

What noise there, ho?

PAULINA.

No noise, my lord; but needful conference
About some gossips for your highness.

LEONTES.

How!
Away with that audacious lady! Antigonus,
I charged thee that she should not come about me:
I knew she would.

ANTIGONUS.

I told her so, my lord,
On your displeasure's peril and on mine,
She should not visit you.

LEONTES.

What, canst not rule her?

PAULINA.

From all dishonesty he can: in this,
Trust it, he shall not rule me.

ANTIGONUS.

La you now, you hear:
When she will take the rein I let her run;
But she'll not stumble.

PAULINA.

Good my liege, I come;
And, I beseech you, hear me, who profess
Myself your loyal servant, your physician,
Your most obedient counsellor, yet that dare
Less appear so in comforting your evils,
Than such as most seem yours: I say, I come
From your good queen.

LEONTES.

Good queen!

PAULINA.

Good queen, my lord,
Good queen; I say good queen;
And would by combat make her good, so were I
A man, the worst about you.

LEONTES.

Force her hence.

PAULINA.

Let him that makes but trifles of his eyes
First hand me: on mine own accord I'll off;
But first I'll do my errand. The good queen,
For she is good, hath brought you forth a daughter;
Here 'tis; commends it to your blessing.

Laying down the child.

LEONTES.

Out!

A mankind witch! Hence with her, out o' door:
A most intelligencing bawd!

PAULINA.

Not so: my lord?
I am as ignorant in that as you
In so entitling me, and no less honest
Than you are mad; which is enough, I'll warrant,
As this world goes, to pass for honest.

LEONTES.

Traitors!
Will you not push her out? Give her the bastard.

Thou dotard! thou art woman-tired, unroosted
By thy dame Partlet here. Take up the bastard;
Take't up, I say; give't to thy crone.

PAULINA.

For ever

Unvenerable be thy hands, if thou
Takest up the princess by that forced baseness
Which he has put upon't!

LEONTES.

He dreads his wife.

PAULINA.

So I would you did; then 'twere past all doubt
You'ld call your children yours.

LEONTES.

A nest of traitors!

ANTIGONUS.

I am none, by this good light.

PAULINA.

Nor I, nor any

But one that's here, and that's himself, for he
The sacred honour of himself, his queen's,
His hopeful son's, his babe's, betrays to slander,
Whose sting is sharper than the sword's; and will not –
For, as the case now stands, it is a curse
He cannot be compell'd to't – once remove
The root of his opinion, which is rotten
As ever oak or stone was sound.

LEONTES.

A callat

Of boundless tongue, who late hath beat her husband
And now baits me! This brat is none of mine;
It is the issue of Polixenes:
Hence with it, and together with the dam
Commit them to the fire!

PAULINA.

It is yours;

And, might we lay the old proverb to your charge,

So like you, 'tis the worse. Behold, my lords,
Although the print be little, the whole matter
And copy of the father, eye, nose, lip,
The trick of's frown, his forehead, nay, the valley,
The pretty dimples of his chin and cheek, his smiles,
The very mould and frame of hand, nail, finger:
And thou, good goddess Nature, which hast made it
So like to him that got it, if thou hast
The ordering of the mind too, 'mongst all colours
No yellow in't, lest she suspect, as he does,
Her children not her own!

LEONTES.
                              A gross hag
And, lozel, thou art worthy to be hang'd,
That wilt not stay her tongue.

ANTIGONUS.
                              Hang all the husbands
That cannot do that feat, you'll leave yourself
Hardly one subject.

LEONTES.
                    Once more, take her hence.

PAULINA.
A most unworthy and unnatural lord
Can do no more.

LEONTES.
                I'll ha' thee burnt.

PAULINA.
                              I care not:
It is an heretic that makes the fire,
Not she which burns in't. I'll not call you tyrant;
But this most cruel usage of your queen,
Not able to produce more accusation
Than your own weak-hinged fancy, something savours
Of tyranny and will ignoble make you,
Yea, scandalous to the world.

LEONTES.
                          On your allegiance,

Out of the chamber with her! Were I a tyrant,
Where were her life? she durst not call me so,
If she did know me one. Away with her!

PAULINA.

I pray you, do not push me; I'll be gone.
Look to your babe, my lord; 'tis yours: Jove send her
A better guiding spirit! What needs these hands?
You, that are thus so tender o'er his follies,
Will never do him good, not one of you.
So, so: farewell; we are gone.

Exit.

LEONTES.

Thou, traitor, hast set on thy wife to this.
My child? away with't! Even thou, that hast
A heart so tender o'er it, take it hence
And see it instantly consumed with fire;
Even thou and none but thou.
For thou set'st on thy wife.

ANTIGONUS.

                                I did not, sir:

AMADIS.

He is not guilty of her coming hither.

LEONTES.

You're liars all.

AMADIS.

Beseech your highness, give us better credit:
We have always truly served you, and beseech you
So to esteem of us, and on our knees we beg,
As recompense of our dear services
Past and to come, that you do change this purpose,
Which being so horrible, so bloody, must
Lead on to some foul issue: we all kneel.

LEONTES.

I am a feather for each wind that blows:
Shall I live on to see this bastard kneel
And call me father? better burn it now
Than curse it then. But be it; let it live.

It shall not neither. You, sir, come you hither;
You that have been so tenderly officious
With Lady Margery, your midwife there,
To save this bastard's life, – for 'tis a bastard,
So sure as this beard's grey, – what will you adventure
To save this brat's life?

ANTIGONUS.

                    Any thing, my lord,
That my ability may undergo
And nobleness impose: at least thus much:
I'll pawn the little blood which I have left
To save the innocent: any thing possible.

LEONTES.

It shall be possible. Swear on thy soul
Thou wilt perform my bidding.

ANTIGONUS.

                    I will, my lord.

LEONTES.

Mark and perform it, see'st thou! for the fail
Of any point in't shall not only be
Death to thyself but to thy lewd-tongued wife,
Whom for this time we pardon. We enjoin thee,
As thou art liege-man to us, that thou carry
This female bastard hence and that thou bear it
To some remote and desert place quite out
Of our dominions, and that there thou leave it,
Where chance may nurse or end it.

ANTIGONUS.

I swear to do this, though a present death
Had been more merciful. Come on, poor babe:
Some powerful spirit instruct the kites and ravens
To be thy nurses! Wolves and bears, they say
Casting their savageness aside have done
Like offices of pity. Sir, be prosperous
In more than this deed does require! And blessing
Against this cruelty fight on thy side,
Poor thing, condemn'd to loss!

Exit with the child.

LEONTES.

No, I'll not rear

Another's issue.

Enter AEGEUM.

AEGEUM.

Please your highness, posts
From those you sent to the Oracle are come
An hour since: Cleomenes and Dion,
Being well arrived from Delphos, are both landed,
Hasting to the court.

AMADIS.

So please you, sir, their speed
Hath been beyond account.

LEONTES.

'Tis good speed; foretells
The great Apollo suddenly will have
The truth of this appear. Prepare you, lords;
Summon a session, that we may arraign
Our most disloyal lady, for, as she hath
Been publicly accused, so shall she have
A just and open trial. While she lives
My heart will be a burden to me. Leave me,
And think upon my bidding.

Exeunt.

ACT THREE

Scene One

A sea-port in Sicilia.

Enter CLEOMENES *and* DION.

CLEOMENES.
    The climate's delicate, the air most sweet,
    Fertile the isle, the temple much surpassing
    The common praise it bears.

DION.
                      I shall report,
    For most it caught me, the celestial habits,
    Methinks I so should term them, and the reverence
    Of the grave wearers. O, the sacrifice!
    How ceremonious, solemn and unearthly
    It was i' the offering!

CLEOMENES.
                But of all, the burst
    And the ear-deafening voice o' the Oracle,
    Kin to Jove's thunder, so surprised my sense.
    That I was nothing.

DION.
               If the event o' the journey
    Prove as successful to the queen, – O be't so! –
    As it hath been to us rare, pleasant, speedy,
    The time is worth the use on't.

CLEOMENES.
                Great Apollo
    Turn all to the best! These proclamations,
    So forcing faults upon Hermione,
    I little like.

DION.
           The violent carriage of it

Will clear or end the business: when the Oracle,
Thus by Apollo's great divine seal'd up,
Shall the contents discover, something rare
Even then will rush to knowledge. Go: fresh horses!
And gracious be the issue!

Exeunt.

Scene Two

A court of justice.

Enter LEONTES, LORDS, *and* OFFICERS.

LEONTES.
This sessions, to our great grief we pronounce,
Even pushes 'gainst our heart: the party tried
The daughter of a king, our wife, and one
Of us too much beloved. Let us be clear'd
Of being tyrannous, since we so openly
Proceed in justice, which shall have due course,
Even to the guilt or the purgation.
Produce the prisoner.

CAPNIO.
It is his highness' pleasure that the queen
Appear in person here in court. Silence!

Enter HERMIONE *guarded;* PAULINA *and* LADIES
attending.

LEONTES.
Read the indictment.

CAPNIO.
(*Reads.*) Hermione, queen to the worthy Leontes, King of
Sicilia, thou art here accused and arraigned of high treason,
in committing adultery with Polixenes, King of Bohemia,
and conspiring with Camillo to take away the life of our
sovereign lord the king, thy royal husband: the pretence
whereof being by circumstances partly laid open, thou,

Hermione, contrary to the faith and allegiance of a true
subject, didst counsel and aid them, for their better safety, to
fly away by night.

HERMIONE.
Since what I am to say must be but that
Which contradicts my accusation and
The testimony on my part no other
But what comes from myself, it shall scarce boot me
To say 'not guilty': mine integrity
Being counted falsehood, shall, as I express it,
Be so received. But thus: if powers divine
Behold our human actions, as they do,
I doubt not then but innocence shall make
False accusation blush and tyranny
Tremble at patience. You, my lord, best know,
Who least will seem to do so, my past life
Hath been as continent, as chaste, as true,
As I am now unhappy; which is more
Than history can pattern, though devised
And play'd to take spectators. For behold me
A fellow of the royal bed, which owe
A moiety of the throne a great king's daughter,
The mother to a hopeful prince, here standing
To prate and talk for life and honour 'fore
Who please to come and hear. For life, I prize it
As I weigh grief, which I would spare: for honour,
'Tis a derivative from me to mine,
And only that I stand for. I appeal
To your own conscience, sir, before Polixenes
Came to your court, how I was in your grace,
How merited to be so; since he came,
With what encounter so uncurrent I
Have strain'd to appear thus: if one jot beyond
The bound of honour, or in act or will
That way inclining, harden'd be the hearts
Of all that hear me, and my near'st of kin
Cry fie upon my grave!

LEONTES.
                I ne'er heard yet
That any of these bolder vices wanted

More impudence to gainsay what they did
Than to perform it first.

HERMIONE.

That's true enough;
Through 'tis a saying, sir, not due to me.

LEONTES.

You will not own it.

HERMIONE.

More than mistress of
Which comes to me in name of fault, I must not
At all acknowledge. For Polixenes,
With whom I am accused, I do confess
I loved him as in honour he required,
With such a kind of love as might become
A lady like me, with a love even such,
So and no other, as yourself commanded:
Which not to have done I think had been in me
Both disobedience and ingratitude
To you and toward your friend, whose love had spoke,
Even since it could speak, from an infant, freely
That it was yours. Now, for conspiracy,
I know not how it tastes; though it be dish'd
For me to try how: all I know of it
Is that Camillo was an honest man;
And why he left your court, the gods themselves,
Wotting no more than I, are ignorant.

LEONTES.

You knew of his departure, as you know
What you have underta'en to do in's absence.

HERMIONE.

Sir,
You speak a language that I understand not:
My life stands in the level of your dreams,
Which I'll lay down.

LEONTES.

Your actions are my dreams;
You had a bastard by Polixenes,
And I but dream'd it. As you were past all shame, –

Those of your fact are so – so past all truth:
Which to deny concerns more than avails; for as
Thy brat hath been cast out, like to itself,
No father owning it, – which is, indeed,
More criminal in thee than it, – so thou
Shalt feel our justice, in whose easiest passage
Look for no less than death.

HERMIONE.

                                        Sir, spare your threats:
The bug which you would fright me with I seek.
To me can life be no commodity:
The crown and comfort of my life, your favour,
I do give lost; for I do feel it gone,
But know not how it went. My second joy
And first-fruits of my body, from his presence
I am barr'd, like one infectious. My third comfort
Starr'd most unluckily, is from my breast,
The innocent milk in its most innocent mouth,
Haled out to murder: myself on every post
Proclaimed a strumpet: with immodest hatred
The child-bed privilege denied, which 'longs
To women of all fashion; lastly, hurried
Here to this place, i' the open air, before
I have got strength of limit. Now, my liege,
Tell me what blessings I have here alive,
That I should fear to die? Therefore proceed.
But yet hear this: mistake me not; no life,
I prize it not a straw, but for mine honour,
Which I would free, if I shall be condemn'd
Upon surmises, all proofs sleeping else
But what your jealousies awake, I tell you
'Tis rigor and not law. Your honours all,
I do refer me to the Oracle:
Apollo be my judge!

AMADIS.

                                This your request
Is altogether just: therefore bring forth,
And in Apollo's name, his Oracle.

Exeunt CAPNIO.

HERMIONE.

The Emperor of Russia was my father:
O that he were alive, and here beholding
His daughter's trial! that he did but see
The flatness of my misery, yet with eyes
Of pity, not revenge!

Re-enter CAPNIO, *with* CLEOMENES *and* DION.

CAPNIO.

You here shall swear,
That you, Cleomenes and Dion, have
Been both at Delphos, and from thence have brought
The seal'd-up Oracle, by the hand deliver'd
Of great Apollo's priest; and that, since then,
You have not dared to break the holy seal
Nor read the secrets in't.

CLEOMENES *and* DION.

All this we swear.

LEONTES.

Break up the seals and read.

CAPNIO.

(*Reads*.) Hermione is chaste; Polixenes blameless; Camillo a
true subject; Leontes a jealous tyrant; his innocent babe truly
begotten; and the king shall live without an heir, if that
which is lost be not found.

AMADIS.

Now blessed be the great Apollo!

HERMIONE.

Praised!

LEONTES.

Hast thou read truth?

CAPNIO.

Ay, my lord; even so
As it is here set down.

LEONTES.

There is no truth at all i' the Oracle:
The sessions shall proceed: this is mere falsehood.

Enter AEGEUM.

AEGEUM.
   My lord the king, the king!

LEONTES.
                    What is the business?

AEGEUM.
   O sir, I shall be hated to report it!
   The prince your son, with mere conceit and fear
   Of the queen's speed, is gone.

LEONTES.
                    How! gone!

AEGEUM.
                                   Is dead.

LEONTES.
   Apollo's angry; and the heavens themselves
   Do strike at my injustice.

HERMIONE *swoons*.

                    How now there!

PAULINA.
   This news is mortal to the queen: look down
   And see what death is doing.

LEONTES.
                    Take her hence:
   Her heart is but o'ercharged; she will recover:
   I have too much believed mine own suspicion:
   Beseech you, tenderly apply to her
   Some remedies for life.

Exeunt PAULINA *and* LADIES, *with* AEGEUM *carrying*
HERMIONE.

                    Apollo, pardon
   My great profaneness 'gainst thine Oracle!
   I'll reconcile me to Polixenes,
   New woo my queen, recall the good Camillo,
   Whom I proclaim a man of truth, of mercy;
   For, being transported by my jealousies

To bloody thoughts and to revenge, I chose
Camillo for the minister to poison
My friend Polixenes: he, most humane
And fill'd with honour, to my kingly guest
Unclasp'd my practice, quit his fortunes here,
Which you knew great, how he glisters
Thorough my rust! and how his piety
Does my deeds make the blacker!

Re-enter PAULINA.

PAULINA.

        Woe the while!
O, cut my lace, lest my heart, cracking it,
Break too.

AMADIS.

    What fit is this, good lady?

PAULINA.

What studied torments, tyrant, hast for me?
What wheels? racks? fires? what flaying? boiling?
In leads or oils? what old or newer torture
Must I receive, whose every word deserves
To taste of thy most worst? Thy tyranny
Together working with thy jealousies,
O, think what they have done
And then run mad indeed, stark mad! for all
Thy bygone fooleries were but spices of it.
That thou betray'dst Polixenes, 'twas nothing;
That did but show thee, of a fool, inconstant
And damnable ingrateful: nor was't much,
Thou wouldst have poison'd good Camillo's honour,
To have him kill a king: poor trespasses,
More monstrous standing by: whereof I reckon
The casting forth to crows thy baby-daughter
To be or none or little; though a devil
Would have shed water out of fire ere done't:
Nor is't directly laid to thee, the death
Of the young prince, whose honourable thoughts,
Thoughts high for one so tender, cleft the heart
That could conceive a gross and foolish sire
Blemish'd his gracious dam: this is not, no,

Laid to thy answer: but the last, – O lords,
When I have said, cry 'woe!' the queen, the queen,
The sweet'st, dear'st creature's dead, and vengeance for't
Not dropp'd down yet.

AMADIS.

                    The higher powers forbid!

PAULINA.

I say she's dead; I'll swear't. If word nor oath
Prevail not, go and see: if you can bring
Tincture or lustre in her lip, her eye,
Heat outwardly or breath within, I'll serve you
As I would do the gods. But, O thou tyrant!
Do not repent these things, for they are heavier
Than all thy woes can stir; therefore betake thee
To nothing but despair. A thousand knees
Ten thousand years together, naked, fasting,
Upon a barren mountain and still winter
In storm perpetual, could not move the gods
To look that way thou wert.

LEONTES.

                    Go on, go on
Thou canst not speak too much; I have deserved
All tongues to talk their bitterest.

AMADIS.

                    Say no more:
Howe'er the business goes, you have made fault
I' the boldness of your speech.

PAULINA.

                    I am sorry for't:
All faults I make, when I shall come to know them,
I do repent. Alas! I have show'd too much
The rashness of a woman: he is touch'd
To the noble heart. What's gone and what's past help
Should be past grief. Now, good my liege
Sir, royal sir, forgive a foolish woman:
The love I bore your queen – lo, fool again! –
I'll speak of her no more, nor of your children;

I'll not remember you of my own lord,
Who is lost too: take your patience to you,
And I'll say nothing.

LEONTES.
                    Thou didst speak but well
When most the truth; which I receive much better
Than to be pitied of thee. Prithee, bring me
To the dead bodies of my queen and son:
One grave shall be for both: upon them shall
The causes of their death appear, unto
Our shame perpetual. Once a day I'll visit
The chapel where they lie, and tears shed there
Shall be my recreation: so long as nature
Will bear up with this exercise, so long
I daily vow to use it. Come and lead me
Unto these sorrows.

Exeunt.

Scene Three

Bohemia. A desert country near the sea.

Enter ANTIGONUS *with a child, and a* MARINER.

ANTIGONUS.
Thou art perfect then, our ship hath touch'd upon
The deserts of Bohemia?

MARINER.
                    Ay, my lord: and fear
We have landed in ill time: the skies look grimly
And threaten present blusters. In my conscience,
The heavens with that we have in hand are angry
And frown upon 's.

ANTIGONUS.
Their sacred wills be done! Go, get aboard;

Look to thy bark: I'll not be long before
I call upon thee.

MARINER.

Make your best haste, and go not
Too far i' the land: 'tis like to be loud weather;
Besides, this place is famous for the creatures
Of prey that keep upon't.

ANTIGONUS.

Go thou away:
I'll follow instantly.

MARINER.

I am glad at heart
To be so rid o' the business.

Exit.

ANTIGONUS.

Come, poor babe:
I have heard, but not believed, the spirits o' the dead
May walk again: if such thing be, thy mother
Appear'd to me last night, for ne'er was dream
So like a waking. To me comes a creature,
Sometimes her head on one side, some another;
I never saw a vessel of like sorrow,
So fill'd and so becoming: in pure white robes,
Like very sanctity, she did approach
My cabin where I lay; thrice bow'd before me,
And gasping to begin some speech, her eyes
Became two spouts: the fury spent, anon
Did this break-from her: 'Good Antigonus,
Since fate, against thy better disposition,
Hath made thy person for the thrower-out
Of my poor babe, according to thine oath,
Places remote enough are in Bohemia,
There weep and leave it crying; and, for the babe
Is counted lost for ever, Perdita,
I prithee, call't. For this ungentle business
Put on thee by my lord, thou ne'er shalt see
Thy wife Paulina more.' And so, with shrieks

She melted into air. Affrighted much,
I did in time collect myself and thought
This was so and no slumber. Dreams are toys:
Yet for this once, yea, superstitiously,
I will be squared by this. I do believe
Hermione hath suffer'd death, and that
Apollo would, this being indeed the issue
Of King Polixenes, it should here be laid,
Either for life or death, upon the earth
Of its right father. Blossom, speed thee well!
There lie, and there thy character: there these;
Which may, if fortune please, both breed thee, pretty,
And still rest thine. The storm begins; poor wretch,
That for thy mother's fault art thus exposed
To loss and what may follow! Weep I cannot,
But my heart bleeds; and most accursed am I
To be by oath enjoin'd to this. Farewell!
The day frowns more and more: thou'rt like to have
A lullaby too rough: I never saw
The heavens so dim by day. Well may I get aboard!
A savage clamour! This is the chase:
I am gone for ever.

Exit, pursued by a bear.

Enter a SHEPHERD.

SHEPHERD.
I would there were no age between ten and three-and-twenty,
or that youth would sleep out the rest; for there is nothing in
the between but getting wenches with child, wronging the
ancientry, stealing, fighting – Hark you now! Would any but
these boiled brains of nineteen and two-and-twenty hunt this
weather? They have scared away two of my best sheep,
which I fear the wolf will sooner find than the master: if any
where I have them, 'tis by the seaside, browsing of ivy. Good
luck, an't be thy will what have we here! Mercy on 's, a
barne a very pretty barne! A boy or a child, I wonder? A
pretty one; a very pretty one: sure, some 'scape: though I am
not bookish, yet I can read waiting-gentlewoman in the
'scape. This has been some stair-work, some trunk-work,

some behind-door-work: they were warmer that got this than the poor thing is here. I'll take it up for pity: yet I'll tarry till my son come; he hallooed but even now. Whoa, ho, hoa!

CLOWN.

Hilloa, loa, loa!

SHEPHERD.

Whoa, hoa!

CLOWN.

Hilloa, loa!

SHEPHERD.

Whoa!

Enter CLOWN.

CLOWN.

Hilloa!

SHEPHERD.

What, art so near? If thou'lt see a thing to talk on when thou art dead and rotten. What ailest thou, man?

CLOWN.

I have seen two such sights, by sea and by land! but I am not to say it is a sea, for it is now the sky: betwixt the firmament and it you cannot thrust a bodkin's point.

SHEPHERD.

Why, boy, how is it?

CLOWN.

I would you did but see how it chafes, how it rages, how it takes up the shore! but that's not the point. O, the most piteous cry of the poor souls! sometimes to see 'em, and not to see 'em; now the ship boring the moon with her main-mast, and anon swallowed with yest and froth, as you'ld thrust a cork into a hogshead. And then for the land-service, to see how the bear tore out his shoulder-bone; how he cried to me for help and said his name was Antigonus, a nobleman. But to make an end of the ship, to see how the sea flap-dragoned it: but, first, how the poor souls roared, and the sea mocked them; and how

the poor gentleman roared and the bear mocked him, both
roaring louder than the sea or weather.

SHEPHERD.
Name of mercy, when was this, boy?

CLOWN.
Now, now: I have not winked since I saw these sights: the
men are not yet cold under water, nor the bear half dined on
the gentleman: he's at it now.

SHEPHERD.
Would I had been by, to have helped the old man!

CLOWN.
I would you had been by the ship side, to have helped her:
there your charity would have lacked footing.

SHEPHERD.
Heavy matters! heavy matters! but look thee here, boy. Now
bless thyself: thou mettest with things dying, I with things
newborn. Here's a sight for thee; look thee, a bearing-cloth
for a squire's child! look thee here; take up, take up, boy;
open't. So, let's see: it was told me I should be rich by the
fairies. This is some changeling: open't. What's within, boy?

CLOWN.
You're a made old man: if the sins of your youth are forgiven
you, you're well to live. Gold! all gold!

SHEPHERD.
This is fairy gold, boy, and 'twill prove so: up with't, keep it
close: home, home, the next way. We are lucky, boy; and to
be so still requires nothing but secrecy. Let my sheep go:
come, good boy, the next way home.

CLOWN.
Go you the next way with your findings. I'll go see if the
bear be gone from the gentleman and how much he hath
eaten: they are never curst but when they are hungry: if there
be any of him left, I'll bury it.

SHEPHERD.
That's a good deed. If thou mayest discern by that which is
left of him what he is, fetch me to the sight of him.

CLOWN.
Marry, will I; and you shall help to put him i' the ground.

SHEPHERD.
'Tis a lucky day, boy, and we'll do good deeds on't.

Exeunt.

Interval.

ACT FOUR

Scene One

Time.

Enter PAULINA *as* TIME, *the chorus.*

TIME.
    I, that please some, try all, both joy and terror
    Of good and bad, that makes and unfolds error,
    Now take upon me, in the name of Time,
    To use my wings. Impute it not a crime
    To me or my swift passage, that I slide
    O'er sixteen years and leave the growth untried
    Of that wide gap, your patience this allowing,
    I turn my glass and give my scene such growing
    As you had slept between: Leontes leaving,
    The effects of his fond jealousies so grieving
    That he shuts up himself, imagine me,
    Gentle spectators, that I now may be
    In fair Bohemia, and remember well,
    I mentioned a son o' the king's, which Florizel
    I now name to you; and with speed so pace
    To speak of Perdita, now grown in grace
    Equal with wondering: what of her ensues
    I list not prophecy; but let Time's news
    Be known when 'tis brought forth. A shepherd's daughter,
    And what to her adheres, which follows after,
    Is the argument of Time. Of this allow,
    If ever you have spent time worse ere now;
    If never, yet that Time himself doth say
    He wishes earnestly you never may.

Exit.

Scene Two

A road near the shepherd's cottage.

Enter AUTOLYCUS, *singing whilst* SHEPHERDS *collect the wool from shorn sheep.*

AUTOLYCUS.
> *When daffodils begin to peer,*
> *With heigh! the doxy over the dale,*
> *Why, then comes in the sweet o' the year;*
> *For the red blood reigns in the winter's pale.*
>
> *The white sheet bleaching on the hedge,*
> *With heigh! the sweet birds, O, how they sing!*
> *Doth set my pugging tooth on edge;*
> *For a quart of ale is a dish for a king.*
>
> *The lark, that tirra-lyra chants,*
> *With heigh! with heigh! the thrush and the jay,*
> *Are summer songs for me and my aunts,*
> *While we lie tumbling in the hay.*

I have served Prince Florizel and in my time wore three-pile; but now I am out of service:

> *But shall I go mourn for that, my dear?*
> *The pale moon shines by night:*
> *And when I wander here and there,*
> *I then do most go right.*
>
> *If tinkers may have leave to live,*
> *And bear the sow-skin budget,*
> *Then my account I well may, give,*
> *And in the stocks avouch it.*

My traffic is sheets; when the kite builds, look to lesser linen. My father named me Autolycus; who being, as I am, littered under Mercury, was likewise a snapper-up of unconsidered trifles. With die and drab I purchased this caparison, and my revenue is the silly cheat. Gallows and knock are too powerful on the highway: beating and hanging are terrors to me: for the life to come, I sleep out the thought of it. A prize! a prize!

Enter CLOWN.

CLOWN.

Let me see: every 'leven wether tods; every tod yields pound
and odd shilling; fifteen hundred shorn – what comes the
wool to?

AUTOLYCUS.

(*Aside*.) If the springe hold, the cock's mine.

CLOWN.

I cannot do't without counters. Let me see; what am I to buy
for our sheep-shearing feast? Three pound of sugar, five
pound of currants, rice, – what will this sister of mine do
with rice? But my father hath made her mistress of the feast,
and she lays it on. I must have saffron to colour the warden
pies; mace; dates? – none, that's out of my note; nutmegs,
seven; a race or two of ginger, but that I may beg; four pound
of prunes, and as many of raisins o' the sun.

AUTOLYCUS.

(*Grovelling on the ground*.) O that ever I was born!

CLOWN.

I' the name of me –

AUTOLYCUS.

O, help me, help me! pluck but off these rags; and then,
death, death!

CLOWN.

Alack, poor soul! thou hast need of more rags to lay on thee,
rather than have these off.

AUTOLYCUS.

O sir, the loathsomeness of them offends me more than the
stripes I have received, which are mighty ones and millions.

CLOWN.

Alas, poor man! a million of beating may come to a great
matter.

AUTOLYCUS.

I am robbed, sir, and beaten; my money and apparel ta'en
from me, and these detestable things put upon me.

CLOWN.

What, by a horseman, or a footman?

AUTOLYCUS.

A footman, sweet sir, a footman.

CLOWN.

Indeed, he should be a footman by the garments he has
left with thee: if this be a horseman's coat, it hath seen very
hot service. Lend me thy hand, I'll help thee: come, lend me
thy hand.

AUTOLYCUS.

O, good sir, tenderly, O!

CLOWN.

Alas, poor soul!

AUTOLYCUS.

O, good sir, softly, good sir! I fear, sir, my shoulder-blade
is out.

CLOWN.

How now! canst stand?

AUTOLYCUS.

(*Picking his pocket.*) Softly, dear sir; good sir, softly. You ha'
done me a charitable office.

CLOWN.

Dost lack any money? I have a little money for thee.

AUTOLYCUS.

No, good sweet sir; no, I beseech you, sir: I have
a kinsman not past three quarters of a mile hence, unto
whom I was going; I shall there have money, or any thing I
want: offer me no money, I pray you; that kills my heart.

CLOWN.

What manner of fellow was he that robbed you?

AUTOLYCUS.

A fellow, sir, that I have known to go about with troll-my-
dames; I knew him once a servant of the prince: but he was
certainly whipped out of the court. I know this man well:

having flown over many knavish professions, He settled only
in rogue: some call him Autolycus.

CLOWN.

Out upon him! prig, for my life, prig: he haunts wakes, fairs
and bear-baitings.

AUTOLYCUS.

Very true, sir; he, sir, he; that's the rogue that put me into
this apparel.

CLOWN.

Not a more cowardly rogue in all Bohemia: if you had but
looked big and spit at him, he'ld have run.

AUTOLYCUS.

I must confess to you, sir, I am no fighter: I am false of heart
that way; and that he knew, I warrant him.

CLOWN.

How do you now?

AUTOLYCUS.

Sweet sir, much better than I was; I can stand and walk: I
will even take my leave of you, and pace softly towards my
kinsman's.

CLOWN.

Shall I bring thee on the way?

AUTOLYCUS.

No, good-faced sir; no, sweet sir.

CLOWN.

Then fare thee well: I must go buy spices for our sheep-
shearing.

AUTOLYCUS.

Prosper you, sweet sir!

Exit CLOWN.

Your purse is not hot enough to purchase your spice. I'll be
with you at your sheep-shearing too: if I make not this cheat
bring out another and the shearers prove sheep, let me be
unrolled and my name put in the book of virtue!

(*Sings*.)
Jog on, jog on, the foot-path way,
And merrily hent the stile-a:
A merry heart goes all the day,
Your sad tires in a mile-a.

Exit.

Scene Three

Bohemia.

Near the shepherd's cottage.

Enter POLIXENES, CAMILLO *and* ARCHIDAMUS.

POLIXENES.
I pray thee, good Camillo, be no more importunate: 'tis a sickness denying thee any thing; a death to grant this.

CAMILLO.
It is fifteen years since I saw my country: though I have for the most part been aired abroad, I desire to lay my bones there. Besides, the penitent king, my master, hath sent for me; to whose feeling sorrows I might be some allay, or I o'erween to think so, which is another spur to my departure.

POLIXENES.
As thou lovest me, Camillo, wipe not out the rest of thy services by leaving me now: the need I have of thee thine own goodness hath made; better not to have had thee than thus to want thee. Of that fatal country, Sicilia, prithee speak no more; whose very naming punishes me with the remembrance of that penitent, as thou callest him, and reconciled king, my brother; whose loss of his most precious queen and children are even now to be afresh lamented. Say to me, when sawest thou the Prince Florizel, my son? Kings are no less unhappy, their issue not being gracious, than they are in losing them when they have approved their virtues.

CAMILLO.

Sir, it is three days since I saw the prince. What his happier affairs may be, are to me unknown: but I have missingly noted, he is of late much retired from court.

POLIXENES.

I have eyes under my service which look upon his removedness; from whom I have this intelligence, that he is seldom from the house close by here of a most homely shepherd; a man, they say, that from very nothing, and beyond the imagination of his neighbours, is grown into an unspeakable estate.

CAMILLO.

I have heard, sir, of such a man, who hath a daughter of most rare note: the report of her is extended more than can be thought to begin from such a cottage.

POLIXENES.

That's likewise part of my intelligence; but, I fear, the angle that plucks our son hither. Not appearing what we are, let us have some question with the shepherd; from whose simplicity I think it not uneasy to get the cause of my son's resort hither. Prithee, be my present partner in this business, and lay aside the thoughts of Sicilia.

CAMILLO.

I willingly obey your command.

POLIXENES.

My best Camillo! We must disguise ourselves.

Exeunt.

Scene Four

The shepherd's cottage.

Enter FLORIZEL *and* PERDITA.

FLORIZEL.
These your unusual weeds to each part of you
Do give a life: no shepherdess, but Flora
Peering in April's front. This your sheep-shearing
Is as a meeting of the petty gods,
And you the queen on't.

PERDITA.
                              Sir, my gracious lord,
To chide at your extremes it not becomes me:
O, pardon, that I name them! Your high self,
The gracious mark o' the land, you have obscured
With a swain's wearing, and me, poor lowly maid,
Most goddess-like prank'd up.

FLORIZEL.
                              I bless the time
When my good falcon made her flight across
Thy father's ground.

PERDITA.
                              Now Jove afford you cause!
To me the difference forges dread; your greatness
Hath not been used to fear. Even now I tremble
To think your father, by some accident,
Should pass this way as you did: O, the Fates!
How would he look, to see his work so noble
Vilely bound up? What would he say? Or how
Should I, in these my borrow'd flaunts, behold
The sternness of his presence?

FLORIZEL.
                              Apprehend
Nothing but jollity. The gods themselves,
Humbling their deities to love, have taken
The shapes of beasts upon them: Jupiter
Became a bull, and bellow'd; the green Neptune
A ram, and bleated; and the fire-robed god,

Golden Apollo, a poor humble swain,
As I seem now. Their transformations
Were never for a piece of beauty rarer,
Nor in a way so chaste, since my desires
Run not before mine honour, nor my lusts
Burn hotter than my faith.

PERDITA.

O, but, sir,
Your resolution cannot hold, when 'tis
Opposed, as it must be, by the power of the king:
You must change this purpose,
Or I my life.

FLORIZEL.

Thou dearest Perdita,
With these forced thoughts, I prithee, darken not
The mirth o' the feast. Or I'll be thine, my fair,
Or not my father's. For I cannot be
Mine own, nor any thing to any, if
I be not thine. To this I am most constant,
Though destiny say no. Your guests are coming:
Lift up your countenance, as it were the day
Of celebration of that nuptial which
We two have sworn shall come.

PERDITA.

O lady Fortune,
Stand you auspicious!

FLORIZEL.
See, your guests approach:
Address yourself to entertain them sprightly,
And let's be red with mirth.

Enter SHEPHERD, CLOWN, MOPSA, DORCAS, *and
others, with* POLIXENES, CAMILLO *and* ARCHIDAMUS
disguised.

SHEPHERD.
Fie, daughter! when my old wife lived, upon
This day she was both pantler, butler, cook,
Both dame and servant; welcomed all, served all;

Would sing her song and dance her turn; now here,
At upper end o' the table, now i' the middle;
On his shoulder, and his; her face o' fire
With labour and the thing she took to quench it,
She would to each one sip. You are retired,
As if you were a feasted one and not
The hostess of the meeting: pray you, bid
These unknown friends to's welcome; for it is
A way to make us better friends, more known.
Come, quench your blushes and present yourself
That which you are, mistress o' the feast.

PERDITA.

(*To* POLIXENES.) Sir, welcome:
It is my father's will I should take on me
The hostess-ship o' the day.
(*To* CAMILLO.) You're welcome, sir.
Give me those flowers there, Dorcas. Reverend sirs,
For you there's rosemary and rue; these keep
Seeming and savour all the winter long:
Grace and remembrance be to you both,
And welcome to our shearing!

POLIXENES.

                              Shepherdess,
A fair one are you – well you fit our ages
With flowers of winter.

PERDITA.

                    Sir, the year growing ancient,
Not yet on summer's death, nor on the birth
Of trembling winter, the fairest flowers o' the season
Are our carnations and streak'd gillyvors,
Which some call nature's bastards: of that kind
Our rustic garden's barren; and I care not
To get slips of them.

POLIXENES.

                    Wherefore, gentle maiden,
Do you neglect them?

PERDITA.

                    For I have heard it said

There is an art which in their piedness shares
With great creating nature.

POLIXENES.

Say there be;
Yet nature is made better by no mean
But nature makes that mean: so, over that art
Which you say adds to nature, is an art
That nature makes. You see, sweet maid, we marry
A gentler scion to the wildest stock,
And make conceive a bark of baser kind
By bud of nobler race: this is an art
Which does mend nature, change it rather, but
The art itself is nature.

PERDITA.

So it is.

POLIXENES.

Then make your garden rich in gillyvors,
And do not call them bastards.

PERDITA.

I'll not put
The dibble in earth to set one slip of them;
No more than were I painted I would wish
This youth should say 'twere well and only therefore
Desire to breed by me. Here's flowers for you;
Hot lavender, mints, savoury, marjoram;
The marigold, that goes to bed wi' the sun
And with him rises weeping: these are flowers
Of middle summer, and I think they are given
To men of middle age. You're very welcome.

CAMILLO.

I should leave grazing, were I of your flock,
And only live by gazing.

PERDITA.

Out, alas!
You'd be so lean, that blasts of January
Would blow you through and through.
Now, my fair'st friend,

I would I had some flowers o' the spring that might
Become your time of day; and yours, and yours,
That wear upon your virgin branches yet
Your maidenheads growing: O Proserpina,
For the flowers now, that frighted thou let'st fall
From Dis's waggon! daffodils,
That come before the swallow dares, and take
The winds of March with beauty; violets dim,
But sweeter than the lids of Juno's eyes
Or Cytherea's breath; pale primroses
That die unmarried, ere they can behold
Bright Phoebus in his strength – a malady
Most incident to maids; bold oxlips and
The crown imperial; lilies of all kinds,
The flower-de-luce being one! O, these I lack,
To make you garlands of, and my sweet friend,
To strew him o'er and o'er!

FLORIZEL.

What, like a corpse?

PERDITA.

No, like a bank for love to lie and play on;
Not like a corpse; or if, not to be buried,
But quick and in mine arms. Come, take your flowers:
Methinks I play as I have seen them do
In Whitsun pastorals: sure this robe of mine
Does change my disposition.

FLORIZEL.

What you do
Still betters what is done. When you speak, sweet.
I'ld have you do it ever: when you sing,
I'ld have you buy and sell so, so give alms,
Pray so; and, for the ordering your affairs,
To sing them too: when you do dance, I wish you
A wave o' the sea, that you might ever do
Nothing but that; move still, still so,
And own no other function.

PERDITA.

O Doricles,

Your praises are too large: but that your youth,
And the true blood which peepeth fairly through't,
Do plainly give you out an unstain'd shepherd,
With wisdom I might fear, my Doricles,
You woo'd me the false way.

FLORIZEL.

                    I think you have
As little skill to fear as I have purpose
To put you to't. But come; our dance, I pray:
Your hand, my Perdita: so turtles pair,
That never mean to part.

PERDITA.

                I'll swear for 'em.

POLIXENES.

This is the prettiest low-born lass that ever
Ran on the green-sward: nothing she does or seems
But smacks of something greater than herself,
Too noble for this place.

CAMILLO.

                He tells her something
That makes her blood look out: good sooth, she is
The queen of curds and cream.

CLOWN.

Come on, strike up!

DORCAS.

Mopsa must be your mistress: marry, garlic,
To mend her kissing with!

MOPSA.

Now, in good time!

CLOWN.

Not a word, a word; we stand upon our manners.
Come, strike up!

Music – Couples Dance.

PERDITA (*singing*).
  Or I'll be thine, my fair

Or not my father's; for I cannot be
Mine own, nor anything to any,
If I be not thine

POLIXENES.

Pray, good shepherd, what fair swain is this
Which dances with your daughter?

SHEPHERD.

They call him Doricles; and boasts himself
To have a worthy feeding: but I have it
Upon his own report and I believe it;
He looks like sooth. He says he loves my daughter:
I think so too; for never gazed the moon
Upon the water as he'll stand and read
As 'twere my daughter's eyes: and, to be plain.
I think there is not half a kiss to choose
Who loves another best.

POLIXENES.

She dances featly.

SHEPHERD.

So she does any thing; though I report it,
That should be silent: if young Doricles
Do light upon her, she shall bring him that
Which he not dreams of.

Enter ARCHIDAMUS *in disguise.*

ARCHIDAMUS.

O master, if you did but hear the pedlar at the door, you
would never dance again after a tabour and pipe; no, the
bagpipe could not move you: he sings several tunes faster
than you'll tell money; he utters them as he had eaten ballads
and all men's ears grew to his tunes.

CLOWN.

He could never come better; he shall come in. I love a ballad
but even too well, if it be doleful matter merrily set down, or
a very pleasant thing indeed and sung lamentably.

ARCHIDAMUS.

He hath songs for man or woman, of all sizes; no milliner

can so fit his customers with gloves: he has the prettiest love-
songs for maids; so without bawdry, which is strange.

POLIXENES.
This is a brave fellow.

CLOWN.
Believe me, thou talkest of an admirable conceited fellow.
Has he any unbraided wares?

ARCHIDAMUS.
He hath ribbons of an the colours i' the rainbow; inkles,
caddisses, cambrics, lawns: why, he sings 'em over as they
were gods or goddesses.

CLOWN.
Prithee bring him in; and let him approach singing.

PERDITA.
Forewarn him that he use no scurrilous words in 's tunes.

Exit ARCHIDAMUS.

CLOWN.
You have of these pedlars, that have more in them
than you'ld think, sister.

PERDITA.
Ay, good brother, or go about to think.

Enter AUTOLYCUS.

AUTOLYCUS (*singing*).
  Lawn as white as driven snow;
  Cyprus black as e'er was crow;
  Gloves as sweet as damask roses;
  Masks for faces and for noses;
  Bugle bracelet, necklace amber,
  Perfume for a lady's chamber;
  Golden quoifs and stomachers,
  For my lads to give their dears:
  Pins and poking-sticks of steel,
  What maids lack from head to heel:
  Come buy of me, come; come buy, come buy;
  Buy lads, or else your lasses cry: Come buy.

CLOWN.

If I were not in love with Mopsa, thou shouldst take no money of me; but being enthralled as I am, it will also be the bondage of certain ribbons and gloves.

MOPSA.

I was promised them against the feast; but they come not too late now.

DORCAS.

He hath promised you more than that, or there be liars.

MOPSA.

He hath paid you all he promised you; may be, he has paid you more, which will shame you to give him again.

CLOWN.

Is there no manners left among maids? will they wear their plackets where they should bear their faces? Is there not milking-time, when you are going to bed, or kiln-hole, to whistle off these secrets, but you must be tittle-tattling before all our guests? 'tis well they are whispering: clamour your tongues, and not a word more.

MOPSA.

I have done. Come, you promised me a tawdry-lace and a pair of sweet gloves.

CLOWN.

Have I not told thee how I was cozened by the way and lost all my money?

AUTOLYCUS.

And indeed, sir, there are cozeners abroad; therefore it behoves men to be wary.

CLOWN.

Fear not thou, man, thou shalt lose nothing here.

AUTOLYCUS.

I hope so, sir; for I have about me many parcels of charge.

CLOWN.

What hast here? ballads?

MOPSA.

Pray now, buy some: I love a ballad in print o' life, for then
we are sure they are true.

AUTOLYCUS.

Here's one to a very doleful tune, how a usurer's wife was
brought to bed of twenty money-bags at a burthen and how
she longed to eat adders' heads and toads carbonadoed.

MOPSA.

Is it true, think you?

AUTOLYCUS.

Very true, and but a month old.

DORCAS.

Bless me from marrying a usurer!

AUTOLYCUS.

Here's the midwife's name to't, one Mistress Tale-porter, and
five or six honest wives that were present. Why should I
carry lies abroad?

MOPSA.

Pray you now, buy it.

CLOWN.

Come on, lay it by: and let's first see moe ballads; we'll buy
the other things anon.

AUTOLYCUS.

Here's another ballad of a fish, that appeared upon the coast
on Wednesday the four-score of April, forty thousand fathom
above water, and sung this ballad against the hard hearts of
maids: it was thought she was a woman and was turned into
a cold fish for she would not exchange flesh with one that
loved her: the ballad is very pitiful and as true.

DORCAS.

Is it true too, think you?

AUTOLYCUS.

Five justices' hands at it, and witnesses more than my pack
will hold.

CLOWN.

Lay it by too: another.

AUTOLYCUS.

This is a merry ballad, but a very pretty one.

MOPSA.

Let's have some merry ones.

AUTOLYCUS.

Why, this is a passing merry one and goes to the tune of
'Two maids wooing a man:' there's scarce a maid westward
but she sings it; 'tis in request, I can tell you.

MOPSA.

We can both sing it: if thou'lt bear a part, thou shalt hear; 'tis
in three parts.

DORCAS.

We had the tune on't a month ago.

AUTOLYCUS.

I can bear my part; you must know 'tis my
occupation; have at it with you.

Song – 'Get You Hence'.

Get you hence, for I must go
Where it fits not you to know.

DORCAS.

Whither?

MOPSA.

   O, whither?

DORCAS.

     Whither?

MOPSA.

It becomes thy oath full well,
Thou to me thy secrets tell.

DORCAS.

Me too, let me go thither.

MOPSA.

Or thou goest to the orange or mill.

DORCAS.

If to either, thou dost ill.

AUTOLYCUS.

Neither.

DORCAS.

What, neither?

AUTOLYCUS.

Neither.

DORCAS.

Thou hast sworn my love to be.

MOPSA.

Thou hast sworn it more to me:
Then whither goest? say, whither?

CLOWN.

We'll have this song out anon by ourselves: my
father and the gentlemen are in sad talk, and we'll
not trouble them. Come, bring away thy pack after
me. Wenches, I'll buy for you both. Pedlar, let's
have the first choice. Follow me, girls.

Music – The Reel Dance.

POLIXENES.

(*To* CAMILLO.) Is it not too far gone? 'Tis time to part them.
(*To* FLORIZEL.) How now, fair shepherd!
Your heart is full of something that does take
Your mind from feasting. Sooth, when I was young
And handed love as you do, I was wont
To load my she with knacks: I would have ransack'd
The pedlar's silken treasury and have pour'd it
To her acceptance; you have let him go
And nothing marted with him.

FLORIZEL.

Old sir, I know
She prizes not such trifles as these are:
The gifts she looks from me are pack'd and lock'd
Up in my heart; which I have given already,
But not deliver'd. O, hear me breathe my life

Before this ancient sir, who, it should seem,
Hath sometime loved! I take thy hand, this hand,
As soft as dove's down and as white as it,
Or Ethiopian's tooth, or the fann'd snow that's bolted
By the northern blasts twice o'er.

POLIXENES.

What follows this?
How prettily the young swain seems to wash
The hand was fair before! I have put you out:
But to your protestation; let me hear
What you profess.

FLORIZEL.

Do, and be witness to 't.

POLIXENES.
And this my neighbour too?

FLORIZEL.

And he, and more
Than he, and men, the earth, the heavens, and all:
That, were I crown'd the most imperial monarch,
Thereof most worthy, were I the fairest youth
That ever made eye swerve, had force and knowledge
More than was ever man's, I would not prize them
Without her love.

POLIXENES.
Fairly offer'd.

CAMILLO.
This shows a sound affection.

SHEPHERD.

But, my daughter,
Say you the like to him?

PERDITA.

I cannot speak
So well, nothing so well; no, nor mean better:
By the pattern of mine own thoughts I cut out
The purity of his.

SHEPHERD.
Take hands, a bargain!
And, friends unknown, you shall bear witness to 't:
I give my daughter to him, and will make
Her portion equal his.

FLORIZEL.
O, that must be
I' the virtue of your daughter. But, come on,
Contract us 'fore these witnesses.

SHEPHERD.
Come, your hand;
And, daughter, yours.

POLIXENES.
Soft, swain, awhile, beseech you;
Have you a father?

FLORIZEL.
I have: but what of him?

POLIXENES.
Knows he of this?

FLORIZEL.
He neither does nor shall.

POLIXENES.
Methinks a father
Is at the nuptial of his son a guest
That best becomes the table. Pray you once more,
Is not your father grown incapable
Of reasonable affairs? is he not stupid
With age and altering rheums? can he speak? hear?
Know man from man? dispute his own estate?
Lies he not bed-rid? and again does nothing
But what he did being childish?

FLORIZEL.
No, good sir;
He has his health and ampler strength indeed
Than most have of his age.

POLIXENES.

By my white beard,
You offer him, if this be so, a wrong
Something unfilial: reason my son
Should choose himself a wife, but as good reason
The father, all whose joy is nothing else
But fair posterity, should hold some counsel
In such a business.

FLORIZEL.

I yield all this;
But for some other reasons, my grave sir,
Which 'tis not fit you know, I not acquaint
My father of this business.

POLIXENES.

Let him know't.

FLORIZEL.
He shall not.

POLIXENES.

Prithee, let him.

FLORIZEL.

No, he must not.

SHEPHERD.
Let him, my son: he shall not need to grieve
At knowing of thy choice.

FLORIZEL.

Come, come, he must not.
Mark our contract.

POLIXENES.
Mark your divorce, young sir,
(*Discovering himself.*) Whom son I dare not call; thou art
    too base
To be acknowledged: thou a sceptre's heir,
That thus affect'st a sheep-hook! Thou old traitor,
I am sorry that by hanging thee I can
But shorten thy life one week. And thou, fresh piece
Of excellent witchcraft, who of force must know
The royal fool thou copest with, –

SHEPHERD.

O, my heart!

POLIXENES.

I'll have thy beauty scratch'd with briers, and made
More homely than thy state. For thee, fond boy,
If I may ever know thou dost but sigh
That thou no more shalt see this knack, as never
I mean thou shalt, we'll bar thee from succession;
Not hold thee of our blood, no, not our kin,
Mark thou my words: follow us to the court.
Thou churl, for this time,
Though full of our displeasure, yet we free thee
From the dead blow of it. And you, enchantment. –
Worthy enough a herdsman: yea, him too,
That makes himself, but for our honour therein,
Unworthy thee, – if ever henceforth thou
These rural latches to his entrance open,
Or hoop his body more with thy embraces,
I will devise a death as cruel for thee
As thou art tender to't.

Exit.

PERDITA.

Even here undone!
I was not much afeard; for once or twice
I was about to speak and tell him plainly,
The selfsame sun that shines upon his court
Hides not his visage from our cottage but
Looks on alike. Will't please you, sir, be gone?
I told you what would come of this: beseech you,
Of your own state take care: this dream of mine, –
Being now awake, I'll queen it no inch farther,
But milk my ewes and weep.

CAMILLO.

Why, how now, father!
Speak ere thou diest.

SHEPHERD.

I cannot speak, nor think
Nor dare to know that which I know. O sir!

You have undone a man of fourscore three,
That thought to fill his grave in quiet, yea,
To die upon the bed my father died,
To lie close by his honest bones: but now
Some hangman must put on my shroud and lay me
Where no priest shovels in dust. O cursed wretch,
That knew'st this was the prince, and wouldst adventure
To mingle faith with him! Undone! undone!
If I might die within this hour, I have lived
To die when I desire.

Exit.

FLORIZEL.
                              Why look you so upon me?
I am but sorry, not afeard; delay'd,
But nothing alter'd: what I was, I am;
More straining on for plucking back, not following
My leash unwillingly.

CAMILLO.
                              Gracious my lord,
You know your father's temper: at this time
He will allow no speech, which I do guess
You do not purpose to him; and as hardly
Will he endure your sight as yet, I fear:
Then, till the fury of his highness settle,
Come not before him.

FLORIZEL.
                              I not purpose it.
I think, Camillo?

CAMILLO.
                              Even he, my lord.

PERDITA.
How often have I told you 'twould be thus!
How often said, my dignity would last
But till 'twere known!

FLORIZEL.
                              Lift up thy looks:
From my succession wipe me, father; I
Am heir to my affection.

CAMILLO.

Be advised.

FLORIZEL.

I am, and by my fancy: if my reason
Will thereto be obedient, I have reason;
If not, my senses, better pleased with madness,
Do bid it welcome.

CAMILLO.

This is desperate, sir.

FLORIZEL.

So call it: but it does fulfil my vow;
I needs must think it honesty. Camillo,
Not for Bohemia, nor the pomp that may
Be thereat glean'd will I break my oath
To this my fair beloved: therefore, I pray you,
As you have ever been my father's honour'd friend,
When he shall miss me, – as, in faith, I mean not
To see him any more, – cast your good counsels
Upon his passion; let myself and fortune
Tug for the time to come. This you may know
And so deliver, I am put to sea
With her whom here I cannot hold on shore;
And most opportune to our need I have
A vessel rides fast by, but not prepared
For this design. What course I mean to hold
Shall nothing benefit your knowledge, nor
Concern me the reporting.

CAMILLO.

O my lord!
I would your spirit were easier for advice,
Or stronger for your need.

FLORIZEL.

Hark, Perdita
(*Drawing her aside*.) I'll hear you by and by.

CAMILLO.

He's irremoveable,
Resolved for flight. Now were I happy, if
His going I could frame to serve my turn,

Save him from danger, do him love and honour,
Purchase the sight again of dear Sicilia
And that unhappy king, my master, whom
I so much thirst to see.

FLORIZEL.
                              Now, good Camillo;
I am so fraught with curious business that
I leave out ceremony.

CAMILLO.
                              Sir, I think
You have heard of my poor services, i' the love
That I have borne your father?
Well, my lord,
If you may please to think I love the king
And through him what is nearest to him, which is
Your gracious self, embrace but my direction:
If your more ponderous and settled project
May suffer alteration, on mine honour,
I'll point you where you shall have such receiving
As shall become your highness; where you may
Enjoy your mistress, marry her,
And, with my best endeavours in your absence,
Your discontenting father strive to qualify
And bring him up to liking.

FLORIZEL.
                              How, Camillo,
May this, almost a miracle, be done?

CAMILLO.
                                        Have you thought on
A place whereto you'll go?

FLORIZEL.
                              Not any yet.

CAMILLO.
Then list to me:
This follows, if you will not change your purpose
But undergo this flight, make for Sicilia,
And there present yourself and your fair princess,
For so I see she must be, 'fore Leontes:

She shall be habited as it becomes
The partner of your bed. Methinks I see
Leontes opening his free arms and weeping
His welcomes forth; asks thee the son forgiveness,
As 'twere i' the father's person; kisses the hands
Of your fresh princess; o'er and o'er divides him
'Twixt his unkindness and his kindness; the one
He chides to hell and bids the other grow
Faster than thought or time.

FLORIZEL.

                       Worthy Camillo,
What colour for my visitation shall I
Hold up before him?

CAMILLO.

                     Sent by the king your father
To greet him and to give him comforts. Sir,
The manner of your bearing towards him, with
What you as from your father shall deliver,
Things known betwixt us three, I'll write you down:
The which shall point you forth at every sitting
What you must say; that he shall not perceive
But that you have your father's bosom there
And speak his very heart.

FLORIZEL.

                  I am bound to you:
There is some sap in this.

CAMILLO.

                 A cause more promising
Than a wild dedication of yourselves
To unpath'd waters, undream'd shores, most certain
To miseries enough; besides you know
Prosperity's the very bond of love,
Whose fresh complexion and whose heart together
Affliction alters.

PERDITA.

              One of these is true:
I think affliction may subdue the cheek,
But not take in the mind.

CAMILLO.

Yea, say you so?

FLORIZEL.

Camillo, preserver of my father, now of me,
The medicine of our house, how shall we do?
We are not furnish'd like Bohemia's son,
Nor shall appear in Sicilia.

CAMILLO.

My lord,
Fear none of this: I think you know my fortunes
Do all lie there: it shall be so my care
To have you royally appointed if
The scene you play were mine. For instance, sir,
That you may know you shall not want, one word.

They talk aside.

Re-enter AUTOLYCUS.

AUTOLYCUS.

Ha, ha! what a fool Honesty is! and Trust, his sworn brother,
a very simple gentleman! I have sold all my trumpery; not a
counterfeit stone, not a ribbon, glass, pomander, brooch,
table-book, ballad, knife, tape, glove, shoe-tie, bracelet,
horn-ring, to keep my pack from fasting: they throng who
should buy first, as if my trinkets had been hallowed and
brought a benediction to the buyer: by which means I saw
whose purse was best in picture; and what I saw, to my good
use I remembered. My clown, who wants but something to
be a reasonable man, grew so in love with the wenches'
song, that he would not stir his pettitoes till he had both tune
and words; which so drew the rest of the herd to me that all
their other senses stuck in ears: you might have pinched a
placket, it was senseless; 'twas nothing to geld a codpiece of
a purse; I could have filed keys off that hung in chains: no
hearing, no feeling, but my sir's song, and admiring the
nothing of it. So that in this time of lethargy I picked and cut
most of their festival purses; and had not the old man come
in with a whoo-bub against his daughter and the king's son
and scared my choughs from the chaff, I had not left a purse
alive in the whole army.

CAMILLO, FLORIZEL, *and* PERDITA *come forward.*

CAMILLO.
Nay, but my letters, by this means being there
So soon as you arrive, shall clear that doubt.

FLORIZEL.
And those that you'll procure from King Leontes –

CAMILLO.
Shall satisfy your father.

PERDITA.
                    Happy be you!
All that you speak shows fair.

CAMILLO.
(*Seeing* AUTOLYCUS.)   Who have we here?
We'll make an instrument of this, omit
Nothing may give us aid.

AUTOLYCUS.
If they have overheard me now, why, hanging.

CAMILLO.
How now, good fellow! why shakest thou so? Fear not, man;
here's no harm intended to thee.

AUTOLYCUS.
I am a poor fellow, sir.

CAMILLO.
Why, be so still; here's nobody will steal that from thee: yet
for the outside of thy poverty we must make an exchange;
therefore discase thee instantly, – thou must think there's a
necessity in't, – and change garments with this gentleman:
though the pennyworth on his side be the worst, yet hold
thee, there's some boot.

AUTOLYCUS.
I am a poor fellow, sir. (*Aside.*) I know ye well enough.

CAMILLO.
Nay, prithee, dispatch: the gentleman is half flayed already.

AUTOLYCUS.
Are you in earnest, sir? (*Aside.*) I smell the trick on't.

FLORIZEL.
Dispatch, I prithee.

AUTOLYCUS.
Indeed, I have had earnest: but I cannot with conscience
take it.

CAMILLO.
Unbuckle, unbuckle.

FLORIZEL *and* AUTOLYCUS *exchange garments.*

Fortunate mistress, – let my prophecy
Come home to ye! – you must retire yourself
Into some covert: take your sweetheart's hat
And pluck it o'er your brows, muffle your face,
Dismantle you, and, as you can, disliken
The truth of your own seeming; that you may –
For I do fear eyes over – to shipboard
Get undescried.

PERDITA.
                              I see the play so lies
That I must bear a part.

CAMILLO.
                              No remedy.
Have you done there?

FLORIZEL.
                              Should I now meet my father,
He would not call me son.

CAMILLO.
                              Nay, you shall have no hat.
(*Giving it to* PERDITA.)
Come, lady, come. Farewell, my friend.

AUTOLYCUS.
Adieu, sir.

FLORIZEL.
O Perdita, what have we twain forgot!
Pray you, a word.

CAMILLO.

 (*Aside*.) What I do next, shall be to tell the king
 Of this escape and whither they are bound;
 Wherein my hope is I shall so prevail
 To force him after: in whose company
 I shall review Sicilia, for whose sight
 I have a woman's longing.

FLORIZEL.

       Fortune speed us!
 Thus we set on, Camillo, to the sea-side.

CAMILLO.

 The swifter speed the better.

 Exeunt FLORIZEL, PERDITA, *and* CAMILLO.

AUTOLYCUS.

 I understand the business, I hear it: to have an open ear, a
 quick eye, and a nimble hand, is necessary for a cut-purse; a
 good nose is requisite also, to smell out work for the other
 senses. I see this is the time that the unjust man doth thrive.
 What an exchange had this been without boot! What a boot
 is here with this exchange! Sure the gods do this year
 connive with us, and we may do any thing extempore. The
 prince himself is about a piece of iniquity, stealing away
 from his father with his clog at his heels: if I thought it were
 a piece of honesty to acquaint the king withal, I would not
 do't: I hold it the more knavery to conceal it; and therein am
 I constant to my profession.

 Re-enter CLOWN *and* SHEPHERD.

 Aside, aside; here is more matter for a hot brain: every lane's
 end, every shop, church, session, hanging, yields a careful
 man work.

CLOWN.

 See, see; what a man you are now! There is no other way but
 to tell the king she's a changeling and none of your flesh and
 blood.

SHEPHERD.

 Nay, but hear me.

CLOWN.
Nay, but hear me.

SHEPHERD.
Go to, then.

CLOWN.
She being none of your flesh and blood, your flesh and blood
has not offended the king; and so your flesh and blood is not
to be punished by him. Show those things you found about
her, those secret things, all but what she has with her: this
being done, let the law go whistle: I warrant you.

SHEPHERD.
I will tell the king all, every word, yea, and his son's pranks
too; who, I may say, is no honest man, neither to his father
nor to me, to go about to make me the king's brother-in-law.

SHEPHERD.
Well, let us to the king: there is that in this fardel will make
him scratch his beard.

AUTOLYCUS.
(*Aside*.) I know not what impediment this complaint may be
to the flight of my master.

CLOWN.
Pray heartily he be at palace.

AUTOLYCUS.
(*Aside*.) Though I am not naturally honest, I am so
sometimes by chance: let me pocket up my pedlar's
excrement. (*Takes off his false beard*.) How now, rustics!
whither are you bound?

SHEPHERD.
To the palace, an it like your worship.

AUTOLYCUS.
Your affairs there, what, with whom, the condition of that
fardel, the place of your dwelling, your names, your ages, of
what having, breeding, and any thing that is fitting to be
known, discover.

CLOWN.
We are but plain fellows, sir.

AUTOLYCUS.

A lie; you are rough and hairy. Let me have no lying: it
becomes none but tradesmen, and they often give us soldiers
the lie.

CLOWN.

Your worship had like to have given us one, if you had not
taken yourself with the manner.

SHEPHERD.

Are you a courtier, an't like you, sir?

AUTOLYCUS.

Whether it like me or no, I am a courtier. I am courtier cap-a-
pe; and one that will either push on or pluck back thy business
there: whereupon I command thee to open thy affair.

SHEPHERD.

My business, sir, is to the king.

AUTOLYCUS.

What advocate hast thou to him?

SHEPHERD.

I know not, an't like you.

CLOWN.

Advocate's the court-word for a pheasant: say you have none.

SHEPHERD.

None, sir; I have no pheasant, cock nor hen.

AUTOLYCUS.

How blessed are we that are not simple men!
Yet nature might have made me as these are,
Therefore I will not disdain.

CLOWN.

This cannot be but a great courtier.

SHEPHERD.

His garments are rich, but he wears them not handsomely.

CLOWN.

He seems to be the more noble in being fantastical: a great
man, I'll warrant; I know by the picking on's teeth.

AUTOLYCUS.

The fardel there? what's i' the fardel? Wherefore that box?

SHEPHERD.

Sir, there lies such secrets in this fardel and box, which none must know but the king; and which he shall know within this hour, if I may come to the speech of him.

AUTOLYCUS.

Age, thou hast lost thy labour.

SHEPHERD.

Why, sir?

AUTOLYCUS.

The king is not at the palace; he is gone aboard a new ship to purge melancholy and air himself: for, if thou beest capable of things serious, thou must know the king is full of grief.

SHEPHERD.

So 'tis said, sir; about his son, that should have married a shepherd's daughter.

AUTOLYCUS.

If that shepherd be not in hand-fast, let him fly: the curses he shall have, the tortures he shall feel, will break the back of man, the heart of monster.

CLOWN.

Think you so, sir?

AUTOLYCUS.

Not he alone shall suffer what wit can make heavy and vengeance bitter.

CLOWN.

Has the old man e'er a son, sir, do you hear. an't like you, sir?

AUTOLYCUS.

He has a son, who shall be flayed alive;
But what talk we of these traitorly rascals, whose miseries are to be smiled at, their offences being so capital? Tell me, for you seem to be honest plain men, what you have to the king: and if it be in man besides the king to effect your suits, here is man shall do it.

CLOWN.
He seems to be of great authority: give him gold; show the inside of your purse to the outside of his hand, and no more ado. Remember 'stoned', and 'flayed alive'.

SHEPHERD.
An't please you, sir, to undertake the business for us, here is that gold I have: I'll make it as much more and leave this young man in pawn till I bring it you.

AUTOLYCUS.
After I have done what I promised?

SHEPHERD.
Ay, sir.

AUTOLYCUS.
Well, give me the moiety.
Walk before toward the sea-side; go on the right hand: I will but look upon the hedge and follow you.

CLOWN.
We are blest in this man, as I may say, even blest.

SHEPHERD.
Let's before as he bids us: he was provided to do us good.

Exeunt SHEPHERD *and* CLOWN.

AUTOLYCUS.
If I had a mind to be honest, I see Fortune would not suffer me: she drops booties in my mouth. I am courted now with a double occasion, gold and a means to do the prince my master good; which who knows how that may turn back to my advancement? I will bring these two moles, these blind ones, aboard him, To him will I present them: there may be matter in it.

Exit.

ACT FIVE

Scene One

A room in Leontes' Palace.

Enter LEONTES, CLEOMENES, DION, *and* PAULINA.

CLEOMENES.
    Sir, you have done enough, and have perform'd
    A saint-like sorrow: no fault could you make,
    Which you have not redeem'd; indeed, paid down
    More penitence than done trespass: at the last,
    Do as the heavens have done, forget your evil;
    With them forgive yourself.

LEONTES.
                 Whilst I remember
    Her and her virtues, I cannot forget
    My blemishes in them, and so still think of
    The wrong I did myself; which was so much,
    That heirless it hath made my kingdom and
    Destroy'd the sweet'st companion that e'er man
    Bred his hopes out of, true.

PAULINA.
                Too true, my lord:
    If, one by one, you wedded all the world,
    Or from the all that are took something good,
    To make a perfect woman, she you kill'd
    Would be unparallel'd.

LEONTES.
            I think so. Kill'd!
    She I kill'd! I did so: but thou strikest me
    Sorely, to say I did; it is as bitter
    Upon thy tongue as in my thought: now, good now,
    Say so but seldom.

CLEOMENES.
                    Not at all, good lady:
    You might have spoken a thousand things that would
    Have done the time more benefit and graced
    Your kindness better.

PAULINA.
                    You are one of those
    Would have him wed again.

DION.
                            If you would not so,
    You pity not the state, nor the remembrance
    Of his most sovereign name; consider little
    What dangers, by his highness' fail of issue,
    May drop upon his kingdom and devour
    Incertain lookers on. What were more holy
    Than to rejoice the former queen is well?
    What holier than, for royalty's repair,
    For present comfort and for future good,
    To bless the bed of majesty again
    With a sweet fellow to't?

PAULINA.
                        There is none worthy,
    Respecting her that's gone. Besides, the gods
    Will have fulfill'd their secret purposes;
    For has not the divine Apollo said,
    Is't not the tenor of his Oracle,
    That King Leontes shall not have an heir
    Till his lost child be found? which that it shall,
    Is all as monstrous to our human reason
    As my Antigonus to break his grave
    And come again to me; who, on my life,
    Did perish with the infant. Care not for issue;
    The crown will find an heir.

LEONTES.
    Good Paulina,
    Who hast the memory of Hermione,
    I know, in honour, O, that ever I

Had squared me to thy counsel! then, even now,
I might have look'd upon my queen's full eyes,
Have taken treasure from her lips –

PAULINA.

And left them
More rich for what they yielded.

LEONTES.

Thou speak'st truth.
No more such wives; therefore, no wife: one worse,
And better used, would make her sainted spirit
Again possess her corpse, and on this stage,
Where we're offenders now, appear soul-vex'd,
And begin, 'Why to me?'

PAULINA.

Had she such power,
She had just cause.

LEONTES.

She had. Fear thou no wife;
I'll have no wife, Paulina.

PAULINA.

Will you swear
Never to marry but by my free leave?

LEONTES.

Never, Paulina; so be blest my spirit!

PAULINA.

Then, good my lords, bear witness to his oath.

CLEOMENES.

You tempt him over-much.

PAULINA.

Unless another,
As like Hermione as is her picture,
Affront his eye.

CLEOMENES.

Good madam, –

PAULINA.

I have done.
Yet, if my lord will marry, – if you will, sir,
No remedy, but you will, – give me the office
To choose you a queen: she shall not be so young
As was your former; but she shall be such
As, walk'd your first queen's ghost, it should take joy
To see her in your arms.

LEONTES.

My true Paulina,
We shall not marry till thou bid'st us.

PAULINA.

That
Shall be when your first queen's again in breath;
Never till then.

Enter CAPNIO.

CAPNIO.

One that gives out himself Prince Florizel,
Son of Polixenes, with his princess, she
The fairest I have yet beheld, desires access
To your high presence.

LEONTES.

What with him? he comes not
Like to his father's greatness: his approach,
So out of circumstance and sudden, tells us
'Tis not a visitation framed, but forced
By need and accident. What train?

CAPNIO.

But few,
And those but mean.

LEONTES.

His princess, say you, with him?

CAPNIO.

Ay, the most peerless piece of earth, I think,
That e'er the sun shone bright on.

LEONTES.

Go, Cleomenes;
Bring them to our embracement. Still, 'tis strange.

Exeunt CLEOMENES *and* DION.

He thus should steal upon us.

PAULINA.

Had our prince,
Jewel of children, seen this hour, he had pair'd
Well with this lord: there was not full a month
Between their births.

LEONTES.

Prithee, no more; cease; thou know'st
He dies to me again when talk'd of: sure,
When I shall see this gentleman, thy speeches
Will bring me to consider that which may
Unfurnish me of reason. They are come.

Re-enter CLEOMENES *and others, with* FLORIZEL *and*
PERDITA.

Your mother was most true to wedlock, prince;
For she did print your royal father off,
Conceiving you: Most dearly welcome!
And your fair princess, – goddess! – O, alas!
I lost a couple, that 'twixt heaven and earth
Might thus have stood begetting wonder as
You, gracious couple, do: and then I lost –
All mine own folly – the society,
Amity too, of your brave father, whom,
Though bearing misery, I desire my life
Once more to look on him.

FLORIZEL.

By his command
Have I here touch'd Sicilia and from him
Give you all greetings that a king, at friend,
Can send his brother: and, but infirmity
Which waits upon worn times hath something seized
His wish'd ability, he had himself
The lands and waters 'twixt your throne and his

Measured to look upon you; whom he loves –
He bade me say so.

LEONTES.

O my brother,
Good gentleman! the wrongs I have done thee stir
Afresh within me, Welcome hither,
As is the spring to the earth. And hath he too
Exposed this paragon to the dreadful Neptune.

FLORIZEL.

Good my lord,
She came from Libya, where the king, her father
That noble honour'd lord, is fear'd and loved
thence, a prosperous south-wind friendly, we have cross'd,
To execute the charge my father gave me
For visiting your highness: my best train
I have from your Sicilian shores dismiss'd;
Who for Bohemia bend, to signify
Not only my success in Libya, sir,
But my arrival and my wife's in safety
Here where we are.

LEONTES.

The blessed gods
Purge all infection from our air whilst you
Do climate here! What might I have been,
Might I a son and daughter now have look'd on,
Such goodly things as you!

Enter AMADIS.

AMADIS.

Most noble sir,
That which I shall report will bear no credit,
Were not the proof so nigh. Please you, great sir,
Bohemia greets you from himself by me;
Desires you to arrest his son, who has –
His dignity and duty both cast off –
Fled from his father, from his hopes, and with
A shepherd's daughter.

LEONTES.

Where's Bohemia? speak.

AMADIS.

Here in your city; I now came from him:
I speak amazedly; and it becomes
My marvel and my message. To your court
Whiles he was hastening, in the chase, it seems,
Of this fair couple, meets he on the way
The father of this seeming lady and
Her brother, having both their country quitted
With this young prince.

FLORIZEL.

Camillo has betray'd me;
Whose honour and whose honesty till now
Endured all weathers.

AMADIS.

Lay't so to his charge:
He's with the king your father.

LEONTES.

Who? Camillo?

AMADIS.

Camillo, sir; I spake with him; who now
Has these poor men in question. Never saw I
Wretches so quake: they kneel, they kiss the earth;
Forswear themselves as often as they speak:
Bohemia stops his ears, and threatens them
With divers deaths in death.

PERDITA.

O my poor father!
The heaven sets spies upon us, will not have
Our contract celebrated.

LEONTES.

You are married?

FLORIZEL.

We are not, sir, nor are we like to be;
The stars, I see, will kiss the valleys first:
The odds for high and low's alike.

LEONTES.

My lord, is this the daughter of a king?

FLORIZEL.

She is, when once she is my wife.

LEONTES.

That 'once' I see by your good father's speed
Will come on very slowly. I am sorry,
Most sorry, you have broken from his liking
Where you were tied in duty, and as sorry
Your choice is not so rich in worth as beauty,
That you might well enjoy her.

FLORIZEL.

Dear, look up:
Though Fortune, visible an enemy,
Should chase us with my father, power no jot
Hath she to change our loves. Beseech you, sir,
Remember since you owed no more to time
Than I do now: with thought of such affections,
Step forth mine advocate; at your request
My father will grant precious things as trifles.

LEONTES.

Would he do so, I'd beg your precious mistress,
Which he counts but a trifle.

PAULINA.

Sir, my liege,
Your eye hath too much youth in't: not a month
'Fore your queen died, she was more worth such gazes
Than what you look on now.

LEONTES.

I thought of her,
Even in these looks I made.
(*To* FLORIZEL.) But your petition
Is yet unanswer'd. I will to your father:
Your honour not o'erthrown by your desires,
I am friend to them and you: upon which errand
I now go toward him; come, good my lord.

Exeunt.

Scene Two

Before Leontes' Palace.

Enter AUTOLYCUS *and* DION.

AUTOLYCUS.
Beseech you, sir, were you present?

DION.
I was by at the opening of the fardel, heard the old shepherd
deliver the manner how he found it: whereupon, after a little
amazedness, we were all commanded out of the chamber; only
this methought I heard the shepherd say, he found the child.

AUTOLYCUS.
I would most gladly know the issue of it.

DION.
I make a broken delivery of the business; but the changes I
perceived in the king and Camillo were very notes of
admiration.

Enter CLEOMENES.

Here comes a gentleman that haply knows more. The news,
Cleomenes?

CLEOMENES.
Nothing but bonfires: the Oracle is fulfilled; the king's
daughter is found: such a deal of wonder is broken out
within this hour that ballad-makers cannot be able to
express it.

Enter AMADIS.

Here comes Amadis: he can deliver you more. How goes it
now, sir? Has the king found his heir?

AMADIS.
Most true, there is such unity in the proofs. The mantle of
Queen Hermione's, her jewel about the neck of it, the letters
of Antigonus found with it which they know to be his
character, and many other evidences proclaim her with all
certainty to be the king's daughter. Did you see the meeting
of the two kings?

CLEOMENES.

No.

AMADIS.

Then have you lost a sight, which was to be seen, cannot be spoken of. There might you have beheld one joy crown another, so and in such manner that it seemed sorrow wept to take leave of them, for their joy waded in tears.

CLEOMENES.

What, pray you, became of Antigonus, that carried hence the child?

AMADIS.

Like an old tale still, he was torn to pieces with a bear: this avouches the shepherd's son; who has not only his innocence, which seems much, to justify him, but a handkerchief and rings of his that Paulina knows.

DION.

What became of his bark and his followers?

AMADIS.

Wrecked the same instant of their master's death and in the view of the shepherd: But O, the noble combat that 'twixt joy and sorrow was fought in Paulina! She had one eye declined for the loss of her husband, another elevated that the Oracle was fulfilled: she lifted the princess from the earth, and so locks her in embracing, as if she would pin her to her heart that she might no more be in danger of losing.

DION.

The dignity of this act was worth the audience of kings and princes; for by such was it acted.

AMADIS.

One of the prettiest touches of all was when, at the relation of the queen's death, with the manner how she came to't bravely confessed and lamented by the king, how attentiveness wounded his daughter; till, from one sign of dolour to another, she did, with an 'Alas', I would fain say, bleed tears, for I am sure my heart wept blood.

DION.

Are they returned to the court?

AMADIS.

No: the princess hearing of her mother's statue, which is in
the keeping of Paulina, – a piece many years in doing by that
rare Italian master, Julio Romano, thither with all greediness
of affection are they gone, and there they intend to sup.

CLEOMENES.

I thought she had some great matter there in hand; for she
hath privately twice or thrice a day, ever since the death of
Hermione, visited that removed house. Shall we thither?

DION.

Who would be thence that has the benefit of access?
Let's along.

Exeunt AMADIS, CLEOMENES *and* DION.

AUTOLYCUS.

Now, had I not the dash of my former life in me, would
preferment drop on my head. I brought the old man and his
son aboard the prince: told him I heard them talk of a fardel
and I know not what: but he at that time, overfond of the
shepherd's daughter, so he then took her to be, who began to
be much sea-sick, and himself little better, extremity of
weather continuing, this mystery remained undiscovered.
But 'tis all one to me; for had I been the finder out of this
secret, it would not have relished among my other discredits.

Enter SHEPHERD *and* CLOWN.

Here come those I have done good to against my will, and
already appearing in the blossoms of their fortune.

SHEPHERD.

Come, boy; I am past moe children, but thy sons and
daughters will be all gentlemen born.

CLOWN.

You are well met, sir. You denied to fight with me this other
day, because I was no gentleman born. See you these
clothes? say you see them not and think me still no
gentleman born: you were best say these robes are not
gentlemen born: give me the lie, do, and try whether I am not
now a gentleman born.

AUTOLYCUS.

I know you are now, sir, a gentleman born.

CLOWN.

Ay, and have been so any time these four hours.

SHEPHERD.

And so have I, boy.

CLOWN.

So you have: but I was a gentleman born before my father; for the king's son took me by the hand, and called me brother; and then the two kings called my father brother; and then the prince my brother and the princess my sister called my father father; and so we wept, and there was the first gentleman-like tears that ever we shed.

SHEPHERD.

We may live, son, to shed many more.

CLOWN.

Ay; or else 'twere hard luck, being in so preposterous estate as we are.

AUTOLYCUS.

I humbly beseech you, sir, to pardon me all the faults I have committed to your worship and to give me your good report to the prince my master.

SHEPHERD.

Prithee, son, do; for we must be gentle, now we are gentlemen.

CLOWN.

Thou wilt amend thy life?

AUTOLYCUS.

Ay, an it like your good worship.

CLOWN.

Give me thy hand: I will swear to the prince thou art as honest a true fellow as any is in Bohemia.

SHEPHERD.

You may say it, but not swear it.

CLOWN.

Not swear it, now I am a gentleman?
I'll swear to the prince thou art a tall fellow of thy hands and
that thou wilt not be drunk; but I know thou art no tall fellow
of thy hands and that thou wilt be drunk: but I'll swear it.

AUTOLYCUS.

I will prove so, sir, to my power.

CLOWN.

Ay, by any means prove a tall fellow:
Hark! the kings and the princes, our kindred, are going to see
the queen's picture. Come, follow us: we'll be thy good
masters.

Exeunt.

Scene Three

A chapel in Paulina's house.

Enter LEONTES, POLIXENES, FLORIZEL, PERDITA,
CAMILLO, PAULINA, LORDS, *and* ATTENDANTS.

LEONTES.

O grave and good Paulina, the great comfort
That I have had of thee!

PAULINA.

What, sovereign sir,
I did not well I meant well.

LEONTES.

O Paulina,
We honour you with trouble: but we came
To see the statue of our queen.

PAULINA.

As she lived peerless,
So her dead likeness, I do well believe,
Excels whatever yet you look'd upon

Or hand of man hath done; therefore I keep it
Lonely, apart. But here it is: prepare
To see the life as lively mock'd as ever
Still sleep mock'd death: behold, and say 'tis well.

PAULINA *draws a curtain, and discovers* HERMIONE
standing like a statue.

I like your silence, it the more shows off
Your wonder: but yet speak; first, you, my liege,
Comes it not something near?

LEONTES.

                  Her natural posture!
Chide me, dear stone, that I may say indeed
Thou art Hermione; or rather, thou art she
In thy not chiding, for she was as tender
As infancy and grace. O, thus she stood,
Even with such life of majesty, warm life,
As now it coldly stands, when first I woo'd her!
I am ashamed: does not the stone rebuke me
For being more stone than it? O royal piece,
There's magic in thy majesty, which has
My evils conjured to remembrance and
From thy admiring daughter took the spirits,
Standing like stone with thee.

PERDITA.

                  And give me leave,
And do not say 'tis superstition, that
I kneel and then implore her blessing. Lady,
Dear queen, that ended when I but began,
Give me that hand of yours to kiss.

PAULINA.

                  O, patience!
The statue is but newly fix'd, the colour's not dry.

CAMILLO.

My lord, your sorrow was too sore laid on,
Which sixteen winters cannot blow away,
So many summers dry; scarce any joy
Did ever so long live; no sorrow
But kill'd itself much sooner.

POLIXENES.

Dear my brother,
Let him that was the cause of this have power
To take off so much grief from you as he
Will piece up in himself.

PAULINA.

Indeed, my lord,
If I had thought the sight of my poor image
Would thus have wrought you, – for the stone is mine –
I'ld not have show'd it.

LEONTES.

Do not draw the curtain.

PAULINA.

No longer shall you gaze on't, lest your fancy
May think anon it moves.

LEONTES.

Let be, let be.
What was he that did make it? See, my lord,
Would you not deem it breathed? and that those veins
Did verily bear blood?

POLIXENES.

Masterly done:
The very life seems warm upon her lip.

LEONTES.

The fixture of her eye has motion in't,
As we are mock'd with art.

PAULINA.

I'll draw the curtain:
My lord's almost so far transported that
He'll think anon it lives.

LEONTES.

O sweet Paulina,
Make me to think so twenty years together!
No settled senses of the world can match
The pleasure of that madness. Let 't alone.

PAULINA.
    I am sorry, sir, I have thus far stirr'd you: but
    I could afflict you farther.

LEONTES.
                                Do, Paulina;
    For this affliction has a taste as sweet
    As any cordial comfort. Still, methinks,
    There is an air comes from her: what fine chisel
    Could ever yet cut breath? Let no man mock me,
    For I will kiss her.

PAULINA.
                        Good my lord, forbear:
    The ruddiness upon her lip is wet;
    You'll mar it if you kiss it,
    Shall I draw the curtain?

LEONTES.
    No, not these twenty years.

PERDITA.
                                So long could I
    Stand by, a looker on.

PAULINA.
                            Either forbear,
    Quit presently the chapel, or resolve you
    For more amazement. If you can behold it,
    I'll make the statue move indeed, descend
    And take you by the hand.

LEONTES.
    What you can make her do,
    I am content to look on: what to speak,
    I am content to hear; for 'tis as easy
    To make her speak as move.

PAULINA.
                                It is required
    You do awake your faith.
    Music, awake her; strike!

    Music.

'Tis time; descend; be stone no more; approach;

HERMIONE *comes down*.

Do not shun her
Until you see her die again; for then
You kill her double. Nay, present your hand:
When she was young you woo'd her; now in age
Is she become the suitor?

LEONTES.
                              O, she's warm!
If this be magic, let it be an art
Lawful as eating.

POLIXENES.
                    She embraces him.

CAMILLO.
She hangs about his neck:
If she pertain to life let her speak too.

POLIXENES.
Ay, and make't manifest where she has lived,
Or how stolen from the dead.

PAULINA.
                              That she is living,
Were it but told you, should be hooted at
Like an old tale: but it appears she lives,
Though yet she speak not. Mark a little while.
Please you to interpose, fair madam: kneel
And pray your mother's blessing. Turn, good lady;
Our Perdita is found.

HERMIONE.
                    You gods, look down
And from your sacred vials pour your graces
Upon my daughter's head! Tell me, mine own.
Where hast thou been preserved? where lived? how found
Thy father's court? for thou shalt hear that I,
Knowing by Paulina that the Oracle
Gave hope thou wast in being, have preserved
Myself to see the issue.

PAULINA.

There's time enough for that;

Go together,
You precious winners all; your exultation
Partake to every one. I, an old turtle,
Will wing me to some wither'd bough and there
My mate, that's never to be found again,
Lament till I am lost.

LEONTES.

O, peace, Paulina!
Thou shouldst a husband take by my consent,
As I by thine a wife: this is a match,
And made between's by vows. Thou hast found mine;
But how, is to be question'd; for I saw her,
As I thought, dead, and have in vain said many
A prayer upon her grave. I'll not seek far –
For him, I partly know his mind – to find thee
An honourable husband. Come, Camillo,
And take her by the hand, whose worth and honesty
Is richly noted and here justified
By us, a pair of kings. Let's from this place.
What! look upon my brother: both your pardons,
That e'er I put between your holy looks
My ill suspicion. This is your son-in-law,
And son unto the king, who, heavens directing,
Is troth-plight to your daughter. Good Paulina,
Lead us from hence, where we may leisurely
Each one demand an answer to his part
Perform'd in this wide gap of time since first
We were dissever'd: hastily lead away.

Exeunt.

www.nickhernbooks.co.uk

 facebook.com/nickhernbooks

 twitter.com/nickhernbooks